THE BROMLEY HOME GUARD

H.M. The King inspecting the Guard of Honour, West Wickham, August 1940.

THE
BROMLEY
HOME
GUARD

A HISTORY OF THE 51st KENT BATTALION

•

by
L.D.V.

The Naval & Military Press Ltd

Published by

The Naval & Military Press Ltd

Unit 5 Riverside, Brambleside
Bellbrook Industrial Estate
Uckfield, East Sussex
TN22 1QQ England

Tel: +44 (0)1825 749494

www.naval-military-press.com
www.nmarchive.com

Printed and bound by CPI Group (UK) Ltd, Croydon, CR0 4YY

*In reprinting in facsimile from the original, any imperfections are inevitably reproduced
and the quality may fall short of modern type and cartographic standards.*

ILLUSTRATIONS

Cover design by Sergeant A. J. Smith, M.G. Company.

PROLOGUE AND
EPILOGUE

THIS is the story of a Home Guard Battalion, in its early days made up almost entirely of men who had served in the last War. As with this Battalion, so with most others. They were the men who said twenty-five years ago : " No more war. We'll see to that. We'll see our sons are kept clear of such destruction and beastliness."

And yet it happened again. Not only were sons involved, but wives, daughters, babies, for science had gone far ahead of civilisation, and only the dead were invulnerable. Almost could they be imagined watching the beastliness and crying :

> We are the Dead, and thus live on ;
> Our flesh the corn of a Flanders plain ;
> The starry flowers on a Turkish cliff ;
> Dust beneath Iraq grain.
> We believed that we died for Liberty's sake—
> The lilac light of an evening shore—
> The song of a thrush—a smiling child
> Asleep on a play-room floor.

Dulce et decorum est pro patria mori is a piece of ancient propaganda. The Nazis have converted it into a religion.

Persuade the world that *pro patria mori* is a disgrace, and there would be no more wars. This may sound like treason to the professional follower of Mars, but it happens to be sanity. If every Home Guard in this country agrees, then there will be no more war. The power to prevent it lies not in Governments, but in the average man. To say that the Nazis caused the trouble is half the truth. They could never have attained power if the average man had asserted himself.

The average Home Guard is the average man. May he make the effort in peace that he made in war.

1940

THE BABY IS BORN

THE policeman's life was not a happy one in the days following Mr. Anthony Eden's broadcast on May 14, 1940. It was the responsibility of the police to deal with applicants who wished to join the L.D.V. The number of applicants was legion; pens, ink, and application forms were only in normal supply. Three thousand volunteers, thirsting for the blood of the Hun, swept down upon Bromley Police Station.

A small committee of local gentlemen had been formed to sort out these applications. Eventually 200 were selected, and notices sent round to the lucky ones to attend at the New Court House on May 25. That afternoon the first issue of denims was made at the Police Station. For the first time, middle-aged men discovered how peculiar they could look in F.S. caps worn too straight and battle blouses too tight, but at least they had a uniform of some sort. It was a definite beginning.

About 1 o'clock in the morning of Sunday, May 26, about 40 of them were suddenly roused by the telephone—to report to the Police Station immediately. Most of them ran there, hoping for the worst. Rifles and ammunition were dealt out, and a short talk on these given to refresh rusty memories. They waited with their weapons in the police library, aching to dash out and fight. Came the dawn, and no developments. The streets of Bromley saw small groups of puzzled men walking home in denims, made more martial by the fact that a number of them had already sewn on to their breasts the military records of their past—all in glorious technicolour.

On the Sunday afternoon there was a meeting of the 200 at the Boys' County School, when the L.D.V., " P " Division, Bromley Group, as it was named, was divided into four companies under the command of Major F. W. L. Hulk. A rota of patrols was formed, and at dusk and dawn bunches of " parashots " were to be seen going about on their lawful occasions. These were the days of a great and enthusiastic innocence. We were quite sure that Huns dropping from the sky would be dead, shot through the middle, before they reached the ground. We were quite sure that enemy tanks, bumping into our improvised barricades of limbers or wooden bars, would be held up and destroyed.

The question of a H.Q. became urgent. Bromley Group moved into 19 East Street, where it has been ever since. Typewriters wer lent and paper bought or borrowed. We began to write officially to each other—" Sow an act, reap a habit."

In these very early stages, strange messages and strange visitors came to the Orderly Room. There was the case of the policeman who rushed in panting, with a written message to state that parachutists had been seen descending over Westmoreland Road. As there was no telephone in the Orderly Room, the place had to be shut while the sole occupant went across to the public telephone box and called on L.D.V.s to go hunting for the parachutists. They turned out to be a flight of pigeons seen by an imaginative old lady. There was the Inventor. He entered late one evening, and suddenly whipped out a gigantic pistol. We thought it was a hold-up, but no; he explained that if parachutists got into buildings it would be difficult to drive them out. This pistol fired a tube of phosphorus, and when it broke it would ignite spontaneously. The buildings concerned would catch fire, and the parachutists would crimson well *have* to come out. His thoughts were gently directed towards the invention of a self-igniting Molotov, possibly the legitimate forerunner of the S.I.P. grenade.

In June, Major Hulk, owing to shortage of time, had to relinquish his appointment, and command of the Group was taken over by Lt.-Col. T. Etchells, D.S.O., M.C. A form of organisation, rough but effective, was developing. We were beginning to realise what the term L.D.V. really meant. Volunteers obviously had to be posted to companies covering their own residential areas, and as Bromley was a biggish place to defend, we needed, and obtained permission, to enlist more men. There was such a wealth of first-class material from which to make a selection, that the process of choosing further recruits became almost embarrassing. Only those between certain ages and with experience of certain arms of the Services were selected, with one exception. An applicant stated on his form that, although without Service experience, he had a wide knowledge of firearms, having been a big-game hunter in South America. Surely a big-game hunter would make a stout soldier ? So he was attested into the Battalion. Months later, when somebody asked him what sort of big game he had shot, he said, " I've never shot anything, but I put that statement down on my application form as I thought it was my only chance of scraping into the Battalion."

Many of the earliest members will recollect how they queued up in the outer rooms at East Street and on 'the stairs, waiting to receive those precious little cards which certified them to be attested members of the L.D.V.

In a sense we were a private Army. Official funds there were none—although the powers-that-be were already issuing many instructions, the carrying out of which inevitably involved expense. However, the net result was to create a spirit the like of which has probably never been known in the history of the world. We became a perfect democracy. Men gave of their money, their labour, their knowledge—each according to his kind. Rank there was none, as we were all volunteers. There seemed nothing incongruous about an ex-Colonel acting under the instructions of an ex-Private.

One of the most Gilbertian examples of this kind occurred one morning when a rather elderly and charming civilian came into the Orderly Room and said that though he felt he was too old to take an active part in the L.D.V., he would very much like to be of some use. " Well," he was told, " there does happen to be one job going—clerk to the Quartermaster. Do you know anything about quartermastering" ? The elderly civilian said he knew a little, and so he was asked to fill up his application form. In the section requiring details of former military service, if any, there appeared the words " 30 years' service in India—Assistant Quartermaster General." These qualifications seeming just about adequate, he was attested, and new recruits found themselves being fitted out by a quartermaster's clerk who wore the C.M.G. and D.S.O.

It was at this period that we were ordered to " defend the roads and approaches to our village." Rifles were few and far between, and shot guns rare. Steel helmets remained either a wistful dream or a privilege of the C.D. Thus the construction of strong posts to protect our remarkably unarmed Forces became vital. Ways and means were considered, and the means obtained from private pockets. Ways were simple. Those who understood such arts as concrete mixing, the erection of timbers, and so forth became the supervisors. The remainder provided the unskilled labour. The stockbroker came back early from the City and wheeled a barrow-load of concrete; the manual worker packed up his job early and came back to tell the stockbroker how damned bad he was at pushing a wheelbarrow. For a period everybody in the Battalion devoted every minute of spare time to this constructional work. It was probably a blessing in disguise, since it gave us a feeling that we were doing something useful, and distracted our minds from a very depressing thought—the lack of arms and ammunition. In due course we had a collection of strong posts of which we were proud.

" A " Company built two of concrete, one at Shortlands (which was opened by the late Lord, Stamp) and the other at the junction of Westmoreland Road and Hayes Lane, which received the adult baptismal name of the King's Post, because it was visited by His Majesty.

"B" Company built one in Hayes Lane, "D" Company one on Bromley Common, which later assumed almost the nature of a club-house, and another near the Crooked Billet; this was so fascinating to the children of the neighbourhood that as fast as material was put into it, they pulled it down.

"C" Company had five posts to their credit, all of them notable for their fine sand-bagging, and one of them for its gallery of Pin-up girls, which could only be seen—fortunately or unfortunately—when the light was switched on.

These labours involved expenditure on materials, use of private cars to convey them, consumption of petrol, wear and tear of civilian clothes and footwear. Nobody complained. In one way it was possibly the best period of the Home Guard. No red tape, no officialdom existed. If we wanted something for the good of the show, we offered to buy it. If the owner refused to sell, we took it darkly by night. These posts were things of our bodies and brains. They became beloved. We would fight in them and die in them if need be. (Some of the more far-seeing and sardonic suggested that we might easily die in them. One crump from a 3-in. mortar shell would have brought scores of tons crashing down on the occupants' heads.)

Then Authority spoke in a rather quiet voice. From June 27 certain Government funds would be available for authorised L.D.V. purposes. The first inch of red tape was creeping towards us. Claims could be made for the use of private cars and for subsistence, the latter being the sum of 1s. 6d. for five hours, to be spent only on food.

It was immediately pointed out by those expert in these matters that beer is food.

This mention of cars brings up the memory of a rather curious incident. A Francis Barnet MC was presented to the Battalion for the use of Volunteer Hawkins (Major R. C. Hawkins, D.S.O.). It was felt that the Government should do something about a motor-cycle used solely for L.D.V. purposes, and letters were sent up "through the usual channels," pathetic letters, angry letters, argumentative letters. In the end, virtue emerged triumphant, and a special licence, the first "G" licence in history, was granted for the motor-cycle.

We had only one grouse—about the shortage of uniforms and

arms. Somehow a man felt that, with only a L.D.V. brassard and a one-eighth share in a rifle, he would not be able to pull his weight when *Der Tag* burst upon us.

On July 4 we changed our name. We became P.1 Battalion, L.D.V. There coincided with this an increase in the issue of denims and rifles. The other weapon was the Molotov cocktail, a bottle filled with crude oil and petrol and ignited by a sort of squib tied to the neck. At the time this grenade was distinctly fashionable, and the Battalion bombers gave an elaborate display in Tiepigs Lane before some of the High and Mighty, which concluded with the destruction of a " German tank," from which alighted a singed and cringing Hitler, impersonated by Volunteer (now Major) E. C. Puplett.

It will be seen from the above that our teething troubles were really no troubles at all, improvisation being the order of the day. Nobody expected official help. We were the masters of our fate, the captains of our souls, and rather cocky. We did not believe in eyewash; perhaps instinctively we were determined to avoid the thing that had nearly been the ruin of this country—the whited sepulchre.

POMP AND CIRCUMSTANCE

On August 10, the Battalions of " P " Division were inspected by H.M. The King on the cricket ground at West Wickham. This early recognition of the L.D.V. had a very valuable effect. For the first time they saw themselves together, and were entitled to be proud of what they saw. The guard of honour was commanded by our present C.O., and " mothered " by an ex-Irish Guardsman, named Marshall, whose very voice might have scared a battalion of Hun paratroops. Demonstrations of the Molotov, etc., were given, and then the Battalions marched past and His Majesty took the salute, on a day so lovely that it seemed impossible to think that invasion was just round the corner.

DUTIES

By now the Battalion had become a fairly closely knit organisation, with the four companies and a dispatch riders' section, all these, of course, providing their own motor or pedal cycles. Company areas had been defined, " A " Company covering part of the town and Shortlands, " B " Company Hayes, " C " Company Downham, Sundridge Park, part of the town and a section of

Bickley, and "D" Company the remainder of Bickley and Bromley Common. Our reponsibilities had been considerably increased. Apart from providing patrols at dusk and dawn, and seeing to it that cars and garages were immobilised, we had started to man observation posts, to keep a general look-out for 'Fifth Columnists, to get to know all about the church bells in the area which would have to be rung in the event of an emergency, and to practise manning our strong posts, which had been completed under the supervision of an ex-Indian Army officer, Lt.-Col. P. Craker, O.B.E., who had an Irish smile only matched by his persuasiveness.

There was also the highly entertaining duty of occasionally blocking the roads leading into Bromley, holding up all pedestrians and traffic, and checking identity cards. Astonishing numbers failed to produce their cards, on one occasion some 300 being found wanting in two hours. Up at D.1 post on Bromley Common, the road was barred every night, and "D" Company personnel learned quite a lot about the frailty of human nature. There was the case of the sentry who stopped a car containing two men and two girls, and asked for their cards. He then said to one girl, "What is your name?" She said, "You can see it for yourself on the card." Being rather a strict sentry, he repeated his question. She looked uncomfortable, and said again, "You can read it on the card." Said the sentry, sternly, "Miss. if you don't answer my question I shall take you along to the Police Station for interrogation." She gave a furtive and nervous glance at her male companion, then leaned across to the sentry and whispered, "I don't want *him* to know!"

As for Fifth Columnists, with their wide and detailed knowledge of everybody in the district, the L.D.V. were able to provide a lot of information on which the Police acted. There were scares and false alarms, but the C.I.D. have stated as a fact that out of every 100 incidents reported, 30 per cent. led to something worth while. As for the Observation Posts, from which we almost hoped to see enemy parachutes descending in the distance, that at the Gaumont Cinema continued to be manned until the summer of 1944. The post at the Sundridge Park Golf Club House, very isolated and hindered by the heavy mists there, had its exciting times. There was a period when the huts nearby were used as a rest camp for A.T.S., and part of the H.G. duty was to be brotherly or fatherly. A third post at Southborough Lane was discontinued as it was felt that the ascent would have been a reasonable test for an old-time sailor or steeplejack.

Word had gone forth that on any air raid alert, companies were to man their strong posts, Battalion H.Q. being at the Police Station. There had been several night alerts, and nothing particular had happened. One brilliant Sunday morning in August we were brought a step nearer to reality. A little after midday the sirens wailed. Companies manned their posts and Battalion H.Q. moved over to the Police Station. We began to hear the stutter of machine-gun fire in the skies, and that dull zooming note of planes diving. There were thuds in the distance, and specks tearing through the air. Presently the police telephones and wireless set were busy with messages. German airmen had been seen baling out in the neighbourhood of Layhams Farm and others behind Sundridge Park. There was a sudden heavy whining and a German plane came across Bromley Common at a very low altitude. We thought it great fun.

A party of officers went out in cars towards Layhams Farm and began to search for the German airmen. Two of our people turned the corner of a hedge and saw a Hun lying on the ground. He was muttering a word which sounded like " Urts." He was told, " Of course it — well 'urts. You shouldn't have come over here," and he was duly picked up and passed over to the R.A.F. Pieces of fuselage, of wing coverings, of parachutes, and bomb containers were scattered about the countryside. At Sundridge Park, " C " Company combed the woods for a human capture. In this they were disappointed, but they had the consolation of collecting various parts of German airplanes, and a very good leather seat—most improperly retained and used by the Company Commander up to this day. Some members of " B " Company swore that the German planes were only about 100 feet up when they dived across. One lucky member of the Company saw something large dropping, threw himself flat, and prayed. The large object bounced, and he found it was a rubber boat, equally useful for sailing on Keston ponds or bathing the baby. " D " Company felt a trifle hurt, because Battalion H.Q. 'phoned them up at their D.1 Post and said something like this : " We suppose you're O.K., as nothing has happened your way." An indignant voice said, " Oh, hasn't it ! We were only standing outside our post watching a plane when it swooped down and machine-gunned us. That's all."

There was another raid in the evening, and the next morning we learned how the German Air Force had been mauled.

To deal with the whole of the Battle of Britain now from the Bromley aspect would be to anticipate. In the succeeding weeks,

[7]

daylight raids became almost banal. In the early stages, people used to take cover. Very soon the attitude of business-as-usual asserted itself, and we even reached the stage of not bothering to look up unless the scrap in the air promised to be extra exciting. For this purpose the flat roofs outside Battalion H.Q. were popular. H.Q. officers would stand there, staring up into the sky at lordly streams of German bombers passing overhead, while the various companies gathered at their posts ready to do anything that might be asked of them. Statistics are dull, but it is interesting to note that during the very many daytime alerts at this stage of the war, the minimum number of personnel manning posts was never less than 100—that during the awkward business hour period—and the time taken to man was in the nature of six or seven minutes.

As everybody knows, Goering's daylight campaign against this country failed, and he then concentrated on night bombing. Here the Battalion was able to be of great assistance. During the first night raid of any consequence on Bromley, incendiaries were dropped in the middle of the town. Personnel of the Battalion cordoned the roads, assisting the police and N.F.S. There were no casualties that night, and we still experienced a sense of thrilled enjoyment. The grimmer work was to come. Soon the wail of the sirens and the crash of bombs became a nightly occurrence. Shrapnel laced the skies. The barrage grew bigger, if still inaccurate, and fell upon the just and unjust alike. Then arose the first serious grievance. Our men were on guard at various points, and they had no steel helmets. To stand in the open in a scanty F.S. cap while jagged lumps fell around was not considered an enjoyable sport, and desperate efforts were made to get more helmets. Possibly the summit of improvisation was reached when, on one noisy night, a figure like a Chinese mandarin was seen to be approaching. It turned out to be a volunteer who had put a dustbin lid on his head, with cords from its edges tied to his waist to keep it in position.

The first land-mine to fall in Bromley was mistaken for a Jerry baling out. The Adjutant and Major Bushell of " P " Zone H.Q., who had gone to visit the Observer Corps, received information that a parachutist was descending in the neighbourhood of Widmore Road. They gripped their revolvers, picked up a few men, and then, splitting up into two parties, went chasing off to capture the so-called parachutist as he alighted. The parachute vanished behind the distant houses, and then the searching parties thought the world had come to an end. This was the land-mine that crashed in Tylney Road.

Later that evening, an officer of the Battalion who had passed the West Kent Golf Course in his car reported that the club-house " didn't seem to be there." He was asked to go out and make sure. It certainly wasn't there. Another land-mine had played havoc.

Any of these raids might have been the prelude to invasion. We were on our toes expecting it. On the night of August 25-26 a warning sounded about 10.30 p.m. Posts were manned. Presently an All Clear was given, but before personnel had started to move homewards, a dramatic message came through from the Observer Corps. They had received it from Fighter Command. The message ran : " An unnatural fog from Yarmouth (Isle of Wight) to Beachy Head. Large enemy convoy near coast—extra vigilance at all places." The atmosphere in the Battalion just crackled. Information was passed on to Zone, and all the Battalions turned out. We spent the night polishing our few cartridges, every moment expecting a call. Nothing happened, and it was not until long after that we were able to link up this alarm with the destruction of the German landing craft—filled with men—by the R.A.F.

During the summer Liaison Officer H. H. Payne had made arrangements with the Observer Corps to allow a member of the Liaison Section to be on duty nightly at the R.O.C. centre. It proved to be a contact of extraordinary value. From then right on until September 1944 one of our members was on duty there every night. His job was to be able to read the R.O.C. Operations Table, and to pass on information to Battalion. This enabled us to gauge the likelihood of detachments of the Battalion being needed to deal with an emergency. The accuracy of the information was almost uncanny. A message of this sort would be received : " About 50 enemy bombers passing over Redhill in the direction of Bromley." Praying that they might lose their way and turn elsewhere, we would hear in a few minutes the heavy beat of their engines and the roar of our A.A. At a later stage information became much more advanced. They would tell us when German planes were piling up on the French coast before crossing the Channel, and we judged whether it was worth while going to bed. Until the H.Q. of the R.O.C. was burned out by enemy action and moved elsewhere, " A " Company used to provide a nightly guard there, whose sentries specialised in the ferocity of their challenge. It became a recognised thing, when approaching these H.Q. at night to stamp heavily and cough with gusto, in order to make sure of avoiding sudden death from one's friends.

Bombs, land-mines and incendiaries continued to rain down through the rest of the year. They became a normal part of life, proving how adaptable is the human race. There was the story of the daylight bomb which landed behind East Street Drill Hall, smashing up a blacksmith's shop, killing the occupant, and blasting a small general shop next door. As the shopkeeper picked her shaken self up, a woman came in and said, " I want two eggs, please." She got them. There was a member of a Company who woke up to find a land-mine, unexploded, reclining in his garden. He went out, collected a friend, and took him down the garden. " Gosh, is that it ? " said the friend, staring. " No, you fool, the thing you're looking at is my prize marrow."

Our first blitz casualty on duty was Lieut. E. W. Lewis. He had just taken his car out of the garage to drive down to a meeting at Battalion H.Q. when a bomb fell in the road immediately in front of him. Temporarily blinded by the splintered windscreen, he groped his way clear of the wrecked car. He suffered very severe injury to the eyes, and was a long while in hospital, but eventually resumed his duties in command of No. 12 platoon.

The Battle of Britain gave rise to the necessity of creating a compassionate fund to help blitzed members of the Battalion. Contributions came in from various sources, and a rough and ready system of dealing with cases was put into effect. The old Spanish motto, " He gives twice who gives quickly," proved its truth. A man who has lost all his immediate possessions is nearly as helpless as a new-born babe. A new uniform and a few pounds handed over quickly made just all the difference. From this Compassionate Fund the Benevolent Fund ultimately developed, and is now on a very substantial basis.

VISITING ROUNDS

The nightly manning of posts produced a new duty for Battalion H.Q. officers, that of visiting rounds. Every night two officers in a car would cruise through the blackout, covering a distance of 20 to 23 miles, to see for themselves that all was well. From one aspect at any rate, all was very well. At some of the posts the catering would have done credit to a pre-war restaurant, and a hungry visiting officer might swallow tea and buns at Sundridge Park, mutton and onion sauce at Bromley Common, beer and sandwiches at Hayes, and cocoa and sausage rolls at the Gaumont.

There were superstitions attached to these visiting rounds. The present C.O., who as second-in-command in those days took his tour of duty, always swore that the Huns aimed a bomb at him whenever he approached the junction of Magpie Hall Lane and Bromley Common. Another visiting officer vowed that his companion had uncanny hearing, and could always pick out the sound of a Jerry pilot releasing the bomb lever.

It is a curious fact that at this stage in the war there were very few fogs of any density, otherwise visiting officers might not have got home in time for breakfast. Some of us still remember an occasion, however, when a black night and a heavy mist played tricks with the then Assistant Adjutant. He had left his companion behind at the Police Station to order fried eggs and coffee (those were the days !) and started to walk through South Street to visit the guard at the Drill Hall and the Electricity Unit. To his great surprise he bumped into a wall, so he turned—but bumped into another wall, and turned again and bumped into yet another wall. Panic seized him. Wherever he moved, walls hit him. He was trapped, he was going mad. Because there was nothing else to do, he shouted for help, and eventually his companion, wondering why he was so long getting back, went along South Street and heard the shouting. It turned out that in the mist the Assistant Adjutant had somehow passed through a gateway and was going round and round inside the courtyard of the Town Hall.

BADGES AND BAUBLES

It is quite certain that in the beginning the Regular Army did not understand the L.D.V. one little bit. The serving soldier failed to grasp how a military organisation could be run without ranks and without rank badges. From a sartorial point of view, we all looked alike—denims, some fitting better than others, and a F.S. cap without a badge. How could a man without any rank, and without actual penal powers, command others without any rank ? In fact, it is possible that the thoughts of the serving soldier went further. How could a man without any rank *know* anything ?

Possibly Higher Authority pondered on these matters in the same way as the serving soldier. The first semi-official badges of rank were red ribbons on the epaulette, three for the Battalion Commander, two for the Assistant Battalion Commander, one for the Adjutant and Company Commanders, and a narrower one for the others. Pre-war chocolate boxes were raided for this purpose. The uninitiated scratched their heads and stared, and made wild guesses. Did the red ribbon signify that we had just been vaccinated, or was it a new kind of uniform doled out to refugee troops from Poland ?

Possibly a braid manufacturer insinuated into the minds of the higher-ups the next rank badge development. This took the form of bands of dark blue braid, three for the Battalion Commander, two for the Assistant Battalion Commander, Company Commanders and Adjutant, and one for the remainder. But in the meanwhile somebody else had worked out a new display of colour which we adopted. The ribbons, some worn along the epaulette and some across, according to the nature of the wearer's appointment, were either light blue or yellow. At least, this method enabled people to distinguish the wearers and tell what appointments they held. Also we began to make use of black chevrons, the wearer of three being known officially as an Assistant Platoon Commander.

Here let us meditate. One of the great differences between the L.D.V. and the Regular Army lay in the fact that, whereas the serving soldier usually hopes for promotion, the L.D.V. quite humanly did his best to avoid it. " Take the first stripe" used to be the saying, " and you are lost." Promotion in the L.D.V. meant extra work; pay, honour and glory there was none.

Further analysis of the situation showed another curious by-product. Although personnel were offered appointments on the basis of their ability, many a first-class man could not accept, owing to business pressure and lack of time. Thus a man who might have made a more than adequate Company Commander in the Regular Forces remained a Private in the L.D.V. No wonder the regular soldier failed to understand, since dislike for eyewash and determination to face facts were the key-notes of the movement. It is as well to be blunt here. In some military quarters there was a tendency to regard the L.D.V. as rather amusing and ignorant amateurs. Young officers or N.C.O.s were sometimes sent to us to lecture or demonstrate, and it often turned out that the audience knew considerably more about the subject than the lecturer.

As regular military control gradually gathered over the L.D.V., the occasional voice of the blimp was heard in the land. It has generally been accepted that a young recruit in the Regular Forces will, more or less, believe anything that is put over by his superiors. But we were not young recruits. Most of us were middle-aged men. Experience and knowledge and discrimination combined to produce a general outlook which was not impressed by what has become commonly known as " blah." It was felt on all sides that the control and administration of the L.D.V. should have been given to those who had had full experience of the L.D.V. We knew that our members were prepared to do anything, providing they were given a reasonable reason, but blind faith, surely, could be the slogan only of those unable to think for themselves ?

Until the King's Inspection on August 10, saluting had been forbidden. After this it crept in, though strictly speaking it re-

*Lt.-Col. T. Etchells,
D.S.O., M.C.*

THE COMMANDING OFFICERS, 1940-1944.

*Lt.-Col. H. W. O'Brien,
M.C., T.D.*

Courtesy Century Photos.

OFFICERS OF THE 51st KENT BATTALION HOME GUARD AND AFFILIATED UNITS

taken on the occasion of the Inspection by Field-Marshal Lord Gort, V.C., September 1944.

Back Row (l. to r.) : Lieut. F. A. Tottem ; Lieut. H. A. Hyde ; Lieut. H. Spurdens ; Lieut. R. J. Sutton ; Capt. F. G. Driskell ; Lieut. F. L. Harris ; Lieut. C. M. Monks ; Lieut. C. A. Monks ; Lieut. R. G. Williams, M.M. ; Lieut. R. F. Camp ; Capt. S. B. Dodman ; Lieut. C. J. Comins, M.C. ; Lieut. W. A. Johnston, M.C. ; Capt. J. Merrill ; Lieut. R. S. Shillingford.

Second Row : Lieut. W. V. Packe, D.S.O. ; Lieut. E. R. Scott ; Lieut. C. W. Willison ; Lieut. F. N. Hillier, M.C. ; Lieut. E. W. Lewis ; Lieut. J. N. M. Campbell ; Lieut. A. E. Filby ; Lieut. E. J. Amos ; Capt. S. D. Clarke ; Lieut. A. H. Waters ; Lieut. S. H. Perry ; Lieut. R. B. Drewsbury ; Lieut. F. C. Hufton ; Lieut. R. B. Rogers ; Lieut. S. F. Bagshaw ; Lieut. F. Whitaker ; Lieut. S. J. G. Croker.

Third Row : Lieut. E. J. Killick ; Lieut. F. C. Notman ; Lieut. S. H. C. Rose ; Lieut. H. J. Starr ; Lieut. A. G. Hancock ; Capt. W. S. Hunt ; Capt. F. G. French, R.A. (Quartermaster) ; Major W. P. Sidney, V.C., M.P. ; Capt. C. Dysart ; Capt. W. Lefeaux ; Capt. P. S. Ayers, M.C. ; Lieut. A. S. Clark ; Lieut. J. N. Carr ; Lieut. L. A. Pettitt ; Capt. W. G. Trend.

Seated : Capt. H. H. Payne, M.C. ; Capt. C. L. Jennings ; Major E. C. Puplett ; Major W. L. Harrild ; Major G. A. Pocock, M.C. ; Capt. F. D. Hoys (Adjutant) ; Lieut.-Col. H. W. O'Brien, M.C., T.D. (Commanding Officer) ; Field-Marshal The Viscount Gort, V.C., G.C.B., D.S.O., M.V.O., M.C., A.D.C. Gen. ; Col. F. W. Chamberlain, C.B.E. (Sector Commander) ; Major H. D. Reynolds, M.C. (Second-in-Command) ; Major F. W. Caswell ; Major G. Menpes, M.C. ; Capt. S. Bayliss Smith ; Capt. F. J. Butcher ; Capt. D. Hogg.

In Front : Lieut. W. Ransom ; Lieut. T. Shergold ; Lieut. H. Pocock ; Lieut. E. D. Walpole ; Lieut. T. W. Sanderson (Assistant Adjutant) ; Lieut. J. Edwards.

Field-Marshal Lord Gort, V.C., Inspecting A Company, September 1944.

*No. 5 Platoon (Lieut. Rose) marching past Sector Commander (Col. F. W. Chamberlain, C.B.E.)
on returning from Battalion Route March to Downe, June 1941.*

At Dī Post.

Courtesy Kentish Times.

Machine Gunners prepare for Action—Browning Machine Gun Drill.

mained illegal until Commissions were granted in 1941. Not that it mattered. Discipline came from within.; A man who wants to do a thing gives no trouble, and that possibly was the very marrow of the L.D.V.

As previously mentioned, the first weeks were occupied with building strong posts. Training as such took a back seat. In any event, we had so little to train with. The construction of the Ant - Tank Line and the issue of new weapons completely altered the situation. The Anti-Tank Line was a kind of static snake, born out of a desperate emergency. It was argued that something to stop or at least to delay enemy tanks would have to be the basis of the defence of London. In a great hurry a survey was made. Where houses were close together it was accepted that these could serve as an Anti-Tank obstacle. In open country such as that at Hayes, an Anti-Tank ditch was dug. In the smaller open spaces, concrete pyramids known as dragons' teeth were erected. On the roads there was a system of sunken sockets in which bent rails were to be placed.

For months we ate, drank and slept the Anti-Tank Line. We had manning exercises. Some thought wistfully of the beautiful strong posts they had built, and regretted having to desert them for this new and unwelcome love of theirs. With all the will in the world, men were bound to find these exercises rather boring. To sit down in one spot with a very limited field of view tended to produce the Maginot Line complex. No doubt it was the only available expedient in a crisis, but most of us will feel very grateful that we were not called upon to fight under these conditions. We almost reached the stage of believing that those who lived outside the Anti-Tank Line were inevitably doomed.

Considering the difficulties of supply, we were a lucky Battalion in the issue of weapons. By September there were sufficient .300 rifles for the issue of one per man. Ammunition was still precious, but a certain amount of firing took place at Bisley and at our own private St. George's range. This little range had received the blessing of the Society of Miniature Rifle Clubs to be used as a range for .22. On the very day when the delegates of the S.M.R.C. came down to the range to approve it, some of our personnel were seen walking in carrying service rifles. Delegates stared at these with startled eyes. Said the then Second-in-Command, our present C.O., " Oh, don't worry, our fellows always carry their rifles with them wherever they go." Many will remember how the rifles arrived from America like truffles in aspic. They needed an immense amount of cleaning, but nobody minded. To possess a rifle in those days was to be a citizen of no mean city.

In the autumn arrived supplies of Browning Automatic Rifles, Vickers M.G.s and Lewis Guns, air type. These latter turned up at 1 o'clock in the morning in the middle of a mighty blitz. They had to be taken into East Street Drill Hall—at that date still suffering from the disadvantages of a glass roof—and checked by the light of a shaded torch. Again, nobody minded. Weapons, and more weapons, was the cry.

Possession of Vickers guns brought about the formation of a new unit within the Battalion—the Machine Gun Company. It was felt that the members of this Company, having to learn a fairly intricate mechanism, should preferably be young. Accordingly, the bulk of it was formed from new and young recruits, with a stiffening of the old guard to act as instructors. This Company grew at an amazing pace, and the men themselves had that type or disregard for the Ten Commandments which often produces a good soldier. It also produces a spot of bother occasionally; but the O.C. M.G. Coy. regarded that as all in a day's work. The R.Q.M.S. of that period kept an enormous Great Dane, which often slept at the entrance to the Q.M.'s stores. Possibly there was a reason for this.

While the M.G. Coy. were stripping locks, mounting guns, and making various hurried clanking noises, the rifle companies were receiving instruction in musketry, Molotovs, and in the Mills grenade, a batch of which had been received. There was also a deal of bayonet fighting under an instructor who had been soldiering before most of us were born—E. D. Walpole. His method was all his own, and very effective. Who will forget that lightning lunge, and the *ee-ee* noise he used to make? Incidentally, one of his pupils who subsequently went into the Navy came back on leave with the information that the Navy had adopted Walpole's method of bayonet fighting. The *ee-ee* sound, hissed in unison, was reckoned to have a tremendous moral effect. Walpole, who had been an instructor at Sandhurst, and handled Generals Montgomery and Alexander as young cadets, brought a popularity to the bayonet at a time when the Regular Army was forgetting its use. There were also classes in First Aid training and Gas. Not many volunteered for First Aid; everybody wanted to destroy, not to mend.

In connection with the Molotov cocktails, a certain most respectable member of a Company got himself into rather an embarrassing position. One day he rang up the Orderly Room and said that he was in a great difficulty. He had something to report, and by reason of its nature he could not possibly pass the information through his Company Commander. Could he come to the Orderly Room and tell his story direct ? As the case sounded peculiar he was told that he could come, but that he would not necessarily be listened to. He duly arrived, and in an awkward manner explained that, as a member of a certain platoon, it was his duty on the siren sounding to go round to the platoon strong post. He had done this —his first occasion—during the previous week, and was the first man to get there. " You can judge what I thought," he went on, " when on rushing in I saw not dozens but literally hundreds of beer bottles ! Now I know there is no harm in drinking beer in reason, but for an operational strong post to be stocked with dozens of gallons of beer like that—well, I think it's just awful." Solemnly he was told to go back to the strong post, open a bottle, and sample its contents. No more was heard from that volunteer.

There were also administration exercises, forerunners of a gigantic volume known as " P " Sector Administrative Instructions, which was subsequently published, and which seemed to embrace every possible H.G. administrative contingency from the cradle to the grave; literally to the grave, for it included instructions on how to bury the dead—the buriers taking great care in disposing of the corpse east and west.

With the increase in arms and general activities, transport became a pressing requirement. A Transport Section, consisting chiefly of D.Rs., started to do its best with little materials but plenty of energy, and the first Battalion truck was built. It had a habit of stopping at awkward moments and also of refusing to start, yet somehow it did its job and was always being over-worked. We also acquired a very handsome ambulance at this time, its one drawback being its tremendous consumption of petrol. The bulk of the work was still being carried out by private cars run under " G " licences.

Regular courses had not yet been put into operation, but a special H.G. course at Osterley Park under the direction of Tom Wintringham had been opened to cater for the rough and ready needs of the H.G. Accommodation was primitive, and equipment scanty, but it was backed by a sense of reality, and those who went on it appreciated how much could be done by the use of determination plus imagination. This Osterley Course eventually materialised into the official No. 1 H.G. School at Denbies, near Dorking.

Looking back at things from a distance, it seems that in those days we were still training as individuals rather than as closely co-ordinated bodies of troops. Nobody thought of tactics. Nobody thought or was allowed to think of anything but the Anti-Tank Line. Some of us had visions of literally fighting on our own doorsteps, sitting in the Anti-Tank Line with our homes a few yards behind. That kind of training was bound to produce an individual tendency.

We carried out a certain amount of drill—a very little—in the new three's formation. Most of us, because of the last war, knew how to march, but spit and polish had to be regarded as a minor matter. There was little time for it. Besides, not much spit and polish could be produced out of denims and badgeless caps.

Two of the Companies, " A " and " C," had to exercise their ingenuity in practising laying imaginary mines in imaginary mine-fields. The effect produced rather suggested rheumatic folk dancers. All of the Companies began to take an interest in camouflage, and to be growingly conscious of the importance of such things as not leaving cars in the open and not gathering in groups. But the whole of training was dominated by the shadow of static defence.

One of the bugbears of the period was the practice of sending messages. Our communications consisted of ordinary G.P.O. lines and D.Rs., and as the higher powers seemed to suffer from a worm-like appetite for information, the communication system invariably became jammed. A Company H.Q. a couple of miles away would try to send through information that " enemy " were in the vicinity. Owing to the floods of messages, this particular one might get held up so long that the enemy paratroops would be sitting in the first house of the Coliseum before Battalion H.Q. heard about them. So, quite early in the proceedings, we began to see that it was the man on the spot who mattered, that the Section Leader and the Platoon Commander were the all-important people in battle. Lt.-Col. Etchells, commanding the Battalion then, used to emphasise this at every opportunity. That his opinions were more than justified has been subsequently proved by the way the Regular Army has gone in for decentralisation, placing such responsibility on and faith in the Battle Squad Leader and Platoon Commander.

One other form of training, more particularly for the officers, was encountered in those early months. The Regular Battalion in the vicinity was the 1st Irish Guards. In an emergency it was the duty of the Irish Guards to man the Anti-Tank Line until such a time as the Battalion was mustered and able to take over from them. On being relieved, the Irish Guards were to move out as a counter-attack force. They were a magnificent battalion, and we were very fortunate to be associated with them for almost two years. It was quite obvious that they appreciated the value of the H.G., and they did all in their power to help us with training.

In October the Battalion Commander, anticipating higher authority by a long, long while, had instituted a system of training programmes. These were invaluable to everybody, and became the basis of everything that mattered. Though they could not be looked upon as light holiday reading, and occasionally a Company Commander, finding the fertility of his imagination drying up and racking his brains for some variety to introduce into the next month's programme, may have cursed the day he was born, there is no doubt about it that this early solid foundation was the secret of success.

ODDITIES

So many things were happening during 1940, many of them happening at the same time, that it seems impossible to set them out in chronological order or even to assemble an account of them under any particular heading. For instance, there was our first Church Parade, which took place on November 10 at the Parish Church, now no longer existing owing to enemy action.

We had managed to secure the services of a military band, but at about 5 o'clock on the Saturday news came through that the band would not be available. Some of us were determined by hook or crook to get hold of a band for the occasion, and after a lot of telephone calls and touring through the blackout, we managed to obtain a band of Irish Pipers.

Because of the weather the Battalion paraded in two halves; one in East Street Drill Hall and the other on the platforms at Bromley North Station. Sunday produced a most dismal and drizzling afternoon. H.G. capes had just been issued, and many of the personnel wore these in lieu of greatcoats. We duly moved off, the Pipers leading with the peculiar lope which has a tempo all its own. It is doubtful if a single man present had ever marched before at this tempo. We found an inevitable impulse to keep each foot hovering in the air in turn to synchronise with the wail of the pipes. This, combined with the sway of H.G. cloaks, produced a rather unusual effect. Odd passers-by in the streets looked, and looked again, perhaps imagining that some strange clan had arrived from Connemara to assist in the war effort.

Mention of cloaks leads us to the question of clothing generally. By now, serge battledress had been issued in reasonable quantities. Greatcoats were still scarce, and had been supplemented by these H.G. cloaks which were of excellent material, but very draughty in breezy weather. Nobody loved them except a certain Scotsman, who used to wrap his cloak around himself and imagine he was on his native heath.

Boots, anklets and cap badges were arriving in reasonable quantities, but such things as shoulder titles and flashes were things of the fairly far future.

What we lacked in clothing and equipment we made up in medal ribbons. Apart from honours—two C.M.G.s and four D.S.O.s were espied in those early months—campaigning ribbons were legion. One of these brought its wearer into an embarrassing situation. He was obviously elderly, and a brilliant array of gongs adorned his chest. One day somebody said to him, " How old are you ? " " Sixty-three," replied he. " That's rather remarkable," said his questioner, pointing at one of his ribbons. " At that rate you must have been seven years old when you served in the Chitral campaign." The Chitral veteran muttered a startled oath. " Oh, Lord, I shouldn't have put that one up." Nobody ever discovered his right age. He turned out to have immense energy and a voice like a bull.

· This reminds us of another veteran, who served as a sergeant in the Q.M. stores until he reverted to civil life, but remained at his H.G. job throughout the war. This was E. M. Mills, who first joined the Army in the late 1880's and still retained his crack marksmanship. He grew younger as he grew older, and will probably be quartermastering and shooting long after the youngest of us has become a great-grandfather.

About this time it occurred to some highly placed officer that our communications in an emergency might break down, and there arose in his mind the wonderful thought of a pigeon service. Pigeons might bring messages from Companies to Battalion, and from Battalion to Zone H.Q. almost in the twinkling of an eye. In preparation for an exercise, a pigeon and a basket was actually delivered at Battalion H.Q., but everybody refused to have anything to do with the poor thing. The exercise took place, and the most important of all the pigeons might have brought honour and glory to the pigeon service but for an untimely but very natural distraction. On being released he saw a lady friend of his on a nearby roof, and dallied. Possibly the best Army pigeons are brought up with an austere outlook. This one was not.

In May 1940, at the suggestion of the Electricity Commissioners, a unit was formed by Captain W. G. Trend, the Borough Electrical Engineer, for the protection of the Bromley undertaking. Sixty-six officers and servants of the department at once responded to the call for volunteers, and by March 1941, the number had increased to 81. Later, owing to recruitment for the Regular Forces and the cancellation of departments, it fell to 46; and remained at that figure until the end. Eventually, as in other districts, it was decided that the unit should come under the command of the C.O. of the local battalion.

At first there was considerable difficulty in obtaining arms and equipment, but the first guard, consisting of one N.C.O. and six men, was mounted on June 28, 1940, and when the Stand Down came, the unit had undertaken no fewer than 1,774 guard mountings, involving 10,267 individual guards. On the adoption of the Government's fire-watching scheme the guard, with the approval of the Commissioners, acted as a fire guard in addition to its other duties, and more than once saved the buildings of the undertaking from destruction by fire.

1941

BATTLE OF BRITAIN

THROUGHOUT the first months of this year the heavy night bombing continued. Bromley having the misfortune to be at the junction of two night flying routes and also on the perimeter of the London A.A. defences, received many a bomb from German pilots who decided it was unwise to fly in any further, got rid of their load, and bolted. There were more land-mines. Our personnel were turned out to cordon roads, and to patrol the shopping centres to prevent looting. One drizzling Saturday evening a hostile plane, hit by A.A. fire, crashed with almost deliberate neatness on two houses in Johnson Road, Bromley Common. Fortunately its bombs did not explode. The pilot, who had baled out, landed close to Sundridge Park Mansion Hotel.

Two members of the Battalion, Volunteers S. W. Anthony (now Corporal), " D " Company, and W. E. Whybrow, " A " Company, who had carried out rescue work in circumstances of great gallantry during air raid incidents, were awarded the M.B.E., and subsequently received their decorations from the King at an Investiture. There were probably many fine instances of H.G. work at this stage that have passed unrecorded, but possibly the most outstanding courage of the whole blitz period was that of Home Guard wives. Night after night, month after month, their husbands went out on duty while they went to their shelters and waited. To stay there listening to the crash of bombs, wondering and yet not knowing, was an almost inhuman test of endurance. Under active conditions of danger it is so much easier to cope with things by having something to do, and in that respect the average Home Guard was better off than his wife. When the ultimate history of this war comes to be written, and everything is seen in its proper perspective, the endurance of the wives of London, or for that matter the women of London, should be an undying example of quiet human courage.

From the point of view of the Battalion, the blitz reached its climax on the night of April 16-17. Though it was not so, it seemed to us that on that night the enemy concentrated his venom against Bromley. From 9 p.m. that night until 4 a.m. next morning high explosives and incendiaries fell steadily. The first big bomb destroyed the Parish Church, and the second wrecked the subsidiary church, St. Marks. A shower of incendiaries raining on the old-fashioned and tindery premises occupied by the Observer Corps gutted the place in a very short while. Members of the Battalion managed, however, to save the invaluable operational table.

Bromley blazed; the water supply ran dry; it looked as if by morning there would be nothing left of the town. Quite early in this ugly night, detachments from Companies had been sent for. A platoon from " C " Company, arriving at Widmore Road before the Fire Brigade could cope with things, raced from house to house and put out dozens of incendiaries before they had got a grip. No. 9 Platoon, operating under Lieut. Willison, made its H.Q. at the Police Station, and did very fine work. Men were posted all over the town, and a regular rota kept. They were taken out to the various places in Battalion trucks driven by members of the Heavy Transport. Some of them saved lives; some of them put out fires; some of them took over the duties of the police, who were overwhelmed with work. Over at East Street Drill Hall incendiaries had fallen on the roof of the magazine, and a party of the M.G. Company, working like cheerful lunatics, dealt with the situation very promptly.

Perhaps special mention should be made of the late Volunteer (Corporal) D. P. Whybrow. At a very grave risk he salved the Salvation Army canteen from a blazing garage. He drove personnel from the Police Station to the various posts; he rescued people from houses smashed by land-mine and drove them to hospital. He was at it all night, and continued to give his services throughout the following day when there was still so much to be done.

Three members of the Battalion were killed by enemy action that night, and four were wounded. Among the former were, Volunteer R. E. Willey, of No. 9 Platoon, on his way to report for duty at the Police Station, and Volunteer R. T. Sharp, who had been attested only that evening.

Up to the end of August, 1944, there had fallen upon the Battalion area about 1,000 H.E.s, scores of thousands of incendiaries and 41 Flying Bombs. Some 29,000 properties had been reported damaged and since the total number in the Borough was about 14,000, this meant that every property, on an average, was hit at least twice. These statistics form a vivid comment on modern war.

FORMATION AND APPOINTMENTS

We were beginning to get organised. Besides the four Rifle Companies, " A," " B," " C," and " D," the M.G. Company and the Electricity and Tanks Units, we now had an H.Q. Platoon, consisting of despatch riders and a Heavy Transport Section, an Intelligence Section, Battalion H.Q., consisting of various officers and O.R., and a Medical Section under the newly appointed M.O., Major Rogers. We also had the nucleus of a Band, starting with a Bandmaster, about half a dozen instrumentalists, a number of instruments, a terrific determination, and hosts of difficulties.

Perhaps it would not be out of place here to anticipate and give a rough outline of the development of the Band. By the summer of 1941 they had become pretty good, playing on ceremonial parades, giving performances in Church, House Gardens, and booking several engagements. They grew and improved, and their fame spread. Throughout 1942 and 1943 their engagements increased in number and importance, and in the latter year they gave a broadcast performance. Their strength by then had increased to forty odd. In the early summer of 1943, on the occasion of the Third H.G. Anniversary, when a big March Past was held in front of H.M. The King, ours was the only Band to parade complete as a Regimental Unit, and the flattering remarks made on all sides were certainly deserved. By 1944 their bookings included many engagements in the L.C.C. Parks, although some of these had to be cancelled subsequently on account of the flying bombs.

There is no doubt about it that the lilting thud of the drums, the blare of brass and the more *sotto voce* tone of the wood-wind were a great asset to the Battalion. The M.G. Company Commander, whose H.Q. was close to the Band room, occasionally tore his hair on practice nights, and ran babbling into the street, but he suffered in a good cause. The Band had the distinction of being the first to play the Abyssinian National Anthem in this country. It was a curious story. The Police had arranged a football match against the Free French Forces, at which the late Princess Tsa Hai, daughter of the Emperor of Abyssinia, had consented to kick off. The authorities asked if our Band would play the Abyssinian National Anthem. We approached the Abyssinian Legation and were told there was only one copy of the score of this Anthem in England, and that it could not be obtained in time. Twenty-four hours before the match the Legation 'phoned to say they had obtained the score. Two young members of the Battalion tore up to the Legation on a motor bike, collected the score, brought it back, and handed it over to Band Sergeant Humphrey, who played it over the telephone on a cornet to the Adjutant. On recovering his senses, the Adjutant said, " Well, do what you can." Sergeant Humphrey sought out the Bandmaster, who spent the night writing out the Band parts. On the Saturday afternoon our Band played the Abyssinian National Anthem. Some of the sardonic spectators suggested that, as nobody knew the tune, nobody was in a position to criticise. However, Princess Tsa Hai quite sincerely said she had never heard it played better.

With our operational role becoming more aggressive, in the early autumn it was decided that all G.S. Battalions should have a Mobile Column. This was to be composed of the younger and fitter personnel, and although cycles and " G " licence cars were to be made available as far as possible to this new unit, the name did not imply that the column would tear about the country on wheels. The nucleus of our column consisted of personnel from the various Companies and was built up subsequently from the more active recruits. In due course members of the column were initiated into the mysteries of the toggle rope, street fighting, and the art of getting about the Battalion area in the quickest possible time. In November another Unit was formed—" E " Company, otherwise the depot Company for training recruits. This Company was a boon and a blessing. From December onwards all men joining the Battalion were posted to " E " Company, where they received basic training and were passed out according to their capacity to learn. Under the experienced eye of Lieut. Walpole and the amusing Irish tongue of Colour-Sergeant Moran, members of " E " Company made the most astonishing progress. Between December 1941 and September 1944 some 1,440 recruits passed through the Company.

With the introduction of Commissions as from February 1, 1941, Battalion affairs were put on a more regular basis (a list of officers of the Battalion is given elsewhere in this Volume). The Home Guard Directorate issued the official Establishment of Warrant Officers and N.C.Os. The platoons were numbered from 1 to 20, with four sections in each platoon, and this formation from an administrative point of view remained throughout the following years, although on the operational side it had to be altered to meet the requirements of battle drill and its mystical passion for threes.

On March 1 our title had changed again. We had become the 51st Kent Battalion, Home Guard, although we were no longer administered by the County of Kent T.A., but by the County of London. Our Regular parent remained the Q.O.R. West Kent Regiment, and the rampant horse still flaunted itself on our caps.

CHANGE OF COMMANL

On April 22, 1941, there was a change in command, Lt.-Col. T. Etchells, D.S.O., M.C., being appointed Second-in-Command of " P " Sector, and Lt.-Col. H. W. O'Brien, M.C., T.D. (until then Second-in-Command of the Battalion) taking over the Colonelcy. The Battalion owed a great debt to Col. Etchells. With his shrewd insight, his drive, and his dominant personality, he had not only set a very high standard, but the Battalion had actually achieved it. His gift for organising and dealing with essentials had put us at least a year ahead of most H.G. Battalions. This may sound immodest, but it happens to be fact. Col. O'Brien, with a long military experience dating from 1913 to 1938, had forgotten more about training than most of us ever expected to know. Again, this put us far ahead of the average Battalion. To the combined gifts of these two Colonels the Battalion owed its reputation.

TRAINING AND WEAPONS

Here the menu became more varied, for which we were thankful. New types of grenade were issued, new weapons fascinated us. We practised with the stuttering Tommy Gun and laughed immoderately at the first sight of a Northover Projector, an animated drainpipe that could do almost anything at short ranges.

The Anti-Tank Line complex had started to lose its grip. Enemy paratroops might be dropped in the open spaces, and it would be better to mop them up before they organised themselves and attacked the Anti-Tank Line. So the phrase "Perimeter Defence" became known in the land. This meant getting out more into the open country, and the consequent development of interest in camouflage and battlecraft generally. The M.G. Company turned its thoughts to long fields of fire and exquisite enfilade positions. They were quite sure their enormous fire power made them more important and deadly than all the rest of us put together. Perhaps they were right.

Of the exercises held during 1941, the two most outstanding were a March to Downe and a 24-hour exercise in mid-summer. The March to Downe was a grand affair. During the interval there the London Scottish gave an anti-gas demonstration and the M.G. Company put on a display of M.G. work. The afternoon was notable for the blazing heat of the sun and the fanatical obstinacy of some of the oldest members of the Battalion, who insisted on marching back despite diplomatic admonitions from their Company Commanders. The 24-hour exercise was a full-dress business, with Companies manning the open spaces, a certain amount of " enemy " action, and the administrative side such as feeding and casualties.

It will always be a mystery how so many H.G. managed to put in all their hours of H.G. training and duties. There was a saying, " Civil occupation first, H.G. training second, everything else nowhere." In many instances the first and second categories must have been reversed. Home Guard " widows " bore it all with remarkable patience. Certainly, this was a strange war. The H.G. put in a long day's work, mostly handicapped by the difficulties of blitz travelling, and then, at a time in the evening when he could be justifiably considered tired out, threw on his uniform and spent several more hours training or on guard. There was a lot of truth in the current saying that if you wanted rest it would be much better to join the Regular Forces.

One quiet night, the M.G. Company guard at the Drill Hall held a Rodeo of their own. They obtained some .22 rifles, started firing in the Miniature Range, tried pot shots at various objects, and then decided that human targets (each other) were more interesting. There was a certain amount of blood and confusion, followed by a

Court of Enquiry, and the casualty concerned subsequently became one of our best boxers. The moral would seem to be—if you want to shine at boxing, get somebody to shoot you in the thigh. While on the subject of violence, mention should be made of " B " Company's method of treating bomb shock. By chance we learned that two sentries on duty at " B " Company post had been injured by a bomb falling nearby. When asked if they were much damaged, the Company Commander said, " Oh, no. One had his trousers blown off and a key driven into his thigh. The other got a knock on the head." " What did you do about it ? " " I took them along to the ' George,' gave them a pint apiece, and put them back on duty."

They say it is a wise man who knows his own hat. This remark may also apply to the rifle. One evening a recruit who had been issued with a rifle but no ammunition stepped into the Miniature Range in the Drill Hall, which used to serve as the Guard Room. He leaned his rifle against the wall, had a gossipy little chat with one of the guards off duty, picked up the rifle and went off home.

In the morning the members of the guard unloaded their rifles under the eye of the N.C.O. To his intense astonishment, one man found that he was already unloaded. He squinted along the barrel, ferreted about in the breech of the magazine, and said, " Well, I never . . ! " or something more pungent. The whole affair seemed to be a first-class mystery. Then somebody started to remember, and after a deal of thinking and deduction it was decided that the recruit who had come into the range the previous evening must have picked up the wrong rifle by mistake. Unfortunately nobody knew the name of the recruit. The situation was full of frightful possibilities, and might have served as a plot for a heart-stopping thriller. Here was some poor, innocent, nameless recruit with a loaded rifle in his house, and unaware of it. There was more head-scratching and desperate thinking. Somebody had a brain wave. With true Sherlock logic, he eliminated all possibilities until there was one name left. A courier went tearing off post haste and rescued the loaded rifle from an unsuspecting bedroom.

Of more serious matters to record during the year, 1941 saw the introduction of P.S.Is., of Proficiency Boards, and of a massive volume known as " P " Zone Administrative Instructions. It is most honestly claimed that any person who absorbed and could act upon the entire contents of this volume could become at least a Brigadier in charge of administration.

Two issues of a Battalion Magazine, entitled, *The Willing*

Horse, were published in 1941. They were of an exceptionally high standard in both form and contents. The short and brilliant life of this publication was brought to an end by the stern edict of the Paper Control.

To mention official feeding arrangements under the heading of Oddities may seem impertinent, but the handling of this matter by the powers that be was so quaint, that it seems difficult to treat it solemnly. In the event of mustering, men were to bring 24 hours' rations. One pictured an opulent member dashing along to his post with a plate of caviare or a 10-lb. salmon under his arm. Outlook on what constitutes a 24-hour ration must, obviously, vary. Some people kept a store of food in a haversack, ready to be snatched up at a moment's notice, and years later, on looking into the haversack, gave one gasp and rushed out for fresh air. The difficulty was overcome by the usual H.G. method—private expenditure and common sense. Platoons formed their own stores. Battalion H.Q. collected a private hoard. Never should manning the Anti-Tank Line and empty stomachs become synonymous phrases.

1942

ADMINISTRATION

ALTHOUGH considerable numbers of the younger members of the Battalion had joined the Regular Forces, we were finding little difficulty in replacing them. One or two Recruiting Marches had been held, including a " Mobile " Demonstration of our various weapons. These were mounted on trucks, and the convoy rolled through the district " showing the flag." In 1942, we reached our maximum strength, 1,560. The consequence was that, when the conditions of service in the Home Guard, which took effect from February 16, were changed by 'the authorities, we felt that the change would mean very little to us in the Battalion. Volunteers now became known officially as Privates, service was compulsory, but for some time the influx of volunteers made it unnecessary for us to ask for a supply of directed men. There were some who suggested that this compulsion and direction of men into the H.G. might alter the whole spirit of the movement. It was not so. When eventually we began to receive batches of directed men, they turned out to be excellent; very many of them had failed to join the H.G. earlier for one reason only—they had not been permitted to do so by their employers.

Our operational role progressed a stage further. Taking their cue from the Russians, the authorities realised that perimeter defence was not sufficient, and the new system of defended localities was put into force. There was closer liaison between companies and platoons, as they appreciated the necessity of relying on each other for support. We were beginning, just beginning, to get " counter-attack minded."

T.E.W.Ts. were held. They provided magnificent opportunities for argument and contradiction. The standard of efficiency· was high.

Strange as it may seem, there were certain people outside the H.G. who honestly queried the value of the force. It was pointed out to them that, but for the H.G., the operations in North Africa could not have taken place. It was essential to keep a powerful garrison in the British Isles, and the H.G. was that garrison. Also, the H.G. was doing a most valuable service to the Regular Army and the Forces generally by providing them with a steady flow of youngsters already well-trained. In the last war the recruit had started at scratch; in this war the recruit was often a very knowledgable young man by the time he joined the Forces. Members of the M.G. Company passing into the R.A.F. quickly became Sergeant Instructors in the Browning Machine Gun. Members of the Rifle Companies soon found themselves being promoted N.C.Os. after transfer to the Army. They re-visited us and told us how grateful they were for the training they had received here. (A roll of those who joined the Services may be seen at the end of this volume. It speaks for itself.)

In the early summer we were lucky enough to have the assistance of a platoon of the Irish Guards for a fortnight. They gave us our first introduction to the platoon in the attack. They gave us pleasant little recipes, such as how to cut a man's head off with a cheese wire, and how to stage a tank ambush. Capt. Vernon of the Irish Guards was reckoned to be one of the finest instructors we had encountered. That this grand Guards Battalion could practise what it preached was proved by subsequent achievements in North Africa and Italy.

Courses had increased in number and value. Personnel went to Denbies, Dorking, Purfleet, Caterham, the Field Cookery Course at Mill Hill, and elsewhere. It says very much for their enthusiasm that many of them scraped seven days out of their civil occupations to spend the time on a training course.

Another innovation was the attachment of personnel to regular units. There is a story of how Cpl. Short, of "D" Company, who had first seen service in the South African War, spent a week attached to the Royal Warwicks. One day the Commander of the Company to which he was attached said, " I think you'd better stay in Camp to-morrow as I am putting my fellows through a particularly strenuous route march." Short said, " That's all right. I'll join in." It is rumoured that the march was so strenuous that one by. one the Company fell out, until only Cpl. Short was left to march back into Camp.

Training on the medical side was exceptionally good. By now, besides the M.O., we had four sub-unit M.O.s, and a Medical Corporal with each platoon. These Corporals, besides their First Aid knowledge, knew all about combatant duties. They craved for cuts to bind and blood to staunch. Almost all of them took the St. John Ambulance Badge.

That astonishing weapon, the Spigot Mortar, emerged in 1942. Its original name had been the Blacker Bombard, which had a distinctly mediaeval touch. It was grotesque to look at, deadly accurate, and a great comfort, the only drawback being that owing to its terrific lethal spread we were unable to fire live spigot bombs, since there was no range in the vicinity safe enough. A range and a target were constructed at Erith, the target being of steel and concrete. The first shot fired demolished the target.

Towards the close of the year Tommy Guns were withdrawn and Stens issued in their place. We liked these. Though possibly they were built of derelict milk tins and broken-down bedsteads, they proved accurate and seemed able to withstand any conditions. If dirt got into them they merely blew themselves clean. As for oil, who cared for oil ?

Being a handy man, the H.G. was not a bit surprised when he found himself issued with a piece of sub-artillery known as the Smith Gun. It had solid wheels, and to the utter disgust of the ex-Artilleryman, was led by the snout. To pull it with a " G " licence car on a greasy road was a sure way of adding grey hairs to the directors of insurance companies. Gun teams were duly trained and later a certain amount of practice was carried out.

The other weapon which appeared in 1942 must have made the late W. Heath Robinson writhe with envy. This was the Fougasse —the dragon that crouched in waiting to belch forth fire on any

SOME "IFS".

A Cartoon from the Battalion Magazine, *The Willing Horse.*

Battalion Transport in the early days.

The Battalion Bombing Range at Sundridge Park. Major Northover's team firing against a Battalion team under Lieut. E. W. Lewis at dummy tanks and infantry.

THE INTELLIGENCE SECTION.

Standing (l. to r.) : Ptes. Whitaker, Hornblow, Muil, L./Cpl. Heaton, Pte. Mackay, Cpl. Rollston, Cpl. Hoblyn, Ptes. Darby, Jarvis, Scott, Brown, Kinghorn, L./Cpl. Ash, M.C., Ptes. Dewey, M.C., Janes, Tosland.
Seated : Sgt. Marston, Capt. H. H. Payne, M.C., Sgt. the Hon. A. Stopford, C.M.G.

Some of the Mobile Column at a colleague's Wedding.

"You reach him down and I'll shoot him"

A "B" Company Dawn Patrol.

Another Cartoon from the Battalion Magazine, *The Willing Horse*

Hun vehicle that passed its way. These Fougasses were installed in certain parts of the Battalion area, and one or two of our personnel came to love them. They were, unfortunately, vulnerable to small boys with inquisitive eyes and restless hands, possessing as they did a certain tempting tube down which it was the greatest sport to drop stones. An inspector of " P " Division had the unhappy duty of seeing to it that nobody tampered with these Fougasses. He caught some small boys interfering with one, gave them a heart-to-heart lecture on "helping the enemy," and finished up by saying, " If you want to pull your weight in this war and squash Hitler, you and your pals should keep a watch on these Fougasses and see that nobody interferes." They must have taken his advice very seriously, because the next time he made a tour of inspection, whenever he approached a Fougasse site, a couple of small boys leapt up from hiding and shouted fiercely, " 'Op it ! "

Films as a method of training had started in a rather dry and unambitious fashion. However, with the co-operation of the cinema world, this method of teaching soldiering grew more and more interesting and effective. Cinemas were put at our disposal for Sunday morning showings, and eventually the film as a means of imparting knowledge and instruction became completely first-class.

It was realised that in a vital emergency many of the C.D. Service might be called upon to handle arms, and numbers of them were given a weapons course by our personnel, as also were many members of the Observer Corps.

Further types of grenade were issued, one of them—the Smoke Grenade—which could be fired from the E.Y. Rifle and Cup Discharger—striking us as a delightful piece of work. We never knew why it was subsequently withdrawn, and nearly wept at its departure.

TRANSPORT

There had been worries on the subject of motor-cycles. Those used by our D.R.s were privately owned, and it became more and more difficult to get them repaired. Somebody whispered to the lordly ones : " Why can't W.D. motor-cycles be given to the H.G. ? " The reply was : " There aren't any available." However, some unknown officer in the Statistics Department, glancing casually through his files, discovered a dump of 10,000 W.D. motor cycles which had been forgotten. Of these we received five. We also received a Utility Truck, two Austin " Fleas," and two Vauxhall cars. They were a boon and a blessing. Besides this official transport we had acquired more private vehicles. Sundridge Park Mansion Hotel presented us with their bus. It had a strong personality. There was only one man in the Battalion who could drive it with any degree of success. It had a habit of biting strangers and going to sleep at street corners. Then there was the truck presented by Capt. Bayliss Smith, and most improperly adapted as a platform for a mobile spigot mortar. It worked.

AFFILIATED UNITS

For various reasons, mainly geographical, detachments of other Battalions came under our wing. The biggest of these was " C " Company of the 44th Lon. (L.P.T.B.) Bn., under Capt. Jennings. They were constantly coming out on exercises with us, and co-operating in every possible way. Nearly all old soldiers, they were tough and good; inclined to speak bad French when exasperated, and invaluable as a counter attack force to deal with any situation that might have arisen in the open spaces of Sundridge Park Golf Course. No. 2 Coy. 19th Lon. (S.S. Gas Coy.) joined us on many training occasions and ceremonial parades, as also did the Bromley Platoon of the 29th C.O.L. (Post Office), under Lieut. Ransom, and the Bromley Platoon of the 23rd C.O.L. (Telephone). The 44th and the 29th subsequently gave us most admirable assistance when the fairly arduous duties of the Task Platoon came into force.

TRANSFERS TO A.A.

The first news that we might have to transfer large numbers of personnel to the A.A. was received with very mixed feelings. As an entity the Battalion was proud of itself, and hated losing good men. Quite naturally, companies had no desire to part with members, many of whom had been with them since the start, but the fact had to be tackled. An order was an order. In consequence everybody took the same attitude—that if the A.A. required our men, they should have the best. At the end of December about a hundred, mainly from " A " and " C " Companies, were transferred to the 71st County of London H.G. H.A.A. Battery to take their rota of service with the regular unit there, an original H.A.C. Battery. Though these men had left us on paper, the link was not broken. They continued to turn up at our various social functions and join with us on our ceremonial parades. It was an example of co-operation at its best. From time to time we accused them of scattering the streets with shrapnel and being more of a menace to ourselves than to the Hun. They had plenty of action during

1943-44, making frightful booming noises, firing hundreds of rounds, and modestly claiming various hits. As the " parent " battalion responsible for supplying replacements for this battery, we continued to transfer personnel from time to time.

Early in the year we held a Battalion Concert at the Boys' County School, the programme being a blend of the Twerps Concert Party and the Battalion Band. Somebody made the accusation that " Poet and Peasant " was our signature tune. In August the Battalion had a Sports Meeting at the Bromley Football Club Ground. This was a roaring success, financially and in every other way. Lieut. Hamlin, Sergt. Bissmire and a Committee from the Companies saw to it that we had numerous side-shows besides the actual sports. The day was notable for the fact that it rained everywhere else except Bromley. Perhaps Lieut. (now Lt.-Col.) Hamlin was strong in prayer.

1943

TRAINING

THE epidemic known as Battle Drill had swept over the body military. Aimed at teaching a man in action what to do, how to do it, and to develop personal responsibility and initiative, it was worked out so that a comparatively new recruit could learn the elements of parade ground drill and tactics at the same time. Naturally, there was some rather comic bewilderment in the early stages until men realised that much of what they were doing was merely symbolic. Squad battle drill involving a few men seemed reasonably simple. Platoon battle drill was also simple when actually carried out on the ground, but illustrated on a blackboard it savoured of a tribal dance devised by Fred Karno. Everywhere could be heard the communal chant, " Down, crawl, observe, sights."

Once we had got over the parade ground stage and turned to the tactical application, everybody grew keen on this new form of training. It meant something. It involved battlecraft, movement, camouflage, individual discrimination. There was a nice offensive spirit about it. Elderly posteriors developed a knack of keeping astonishingly flat. Exercises assumed a heartening realism. To approach an " enemy " position, supported by a fusillade of cracker blank, and to charge in finally with a shower of thunder flashes made everybody feel younger. We eventually reached the exalted stage of the company in the attack, with appropriate noises.

Since it was now the job of the H.G. to go out and look for a fight if necessary, instead of sitting down waiting to be hit, our operational role had acquired a more advanced technique.* Mustering exercises were held. On receipt of the summons to muster, men flocked to their Company H.Q., the senior on the spot appointing sentries, forming personnel into battle squads, and so forth. This meant that any member of the H.G. might find himself the first to arrive at the mustering R/V, with attendant responsibilities. We were faintly reminded of the dutiful householder at night, who puts out the cat and the milk bottles, arranges the fireguard, turns off the lights, and so on.

We practised street fighting, particularly in a row of blitzed houses at Lewisham, where an " enemy " fought with guile and booby traps. On one or two of these occasions we brought in the assistance of Sergt. Gore, who, as a plastic artist, was able to make up the most revolting-looking wounds. There was a Sunday morning when two policemen, sent along by the local Superintendent, who had been advised of our exercise, stood watching. Inside one of the houses, an umpire had made a bad casualty and handed him over to Sergt. Gore, who built up on his arm an artistic and frightful crimson wound. The casualty emerged from the house. The younger of the two policemen looked and looked again, turned green and swayed. His companion led him away, and our laughter held up operations for a minute.

Embussing and debussing were practised. The second stroutest officer in the Battalion demonstrated how to bounce when falling off the back of a truck. We had miniature night attacks. On one of these the instructor, who had most earnestly warned members of the course about shielding their eyes from any light, stared at a searchlight that happened to spring up, and promptly lost himself while everybody else went confidently ahead.

With better facilities we had plenty of weapon training. Besides the local ranges there were those at Purfleet, Milton, Shoreham and Westerham. There is no doubt about it that in the earlier days lack of suitable ranges had penalised the shooting standard of the H.G. The introduction of the War Course and increased range facilities were a great help.

As regards bombing we were lucky to have our own private range—Sundridge Park. Here, after every live practice, hordes of children from the neighbouring estate used to swoop down like vultures for souvenirs. Their capacity for removing things was marvellous. We fully believe they would have made off with a heavy tank had we left one there. Some of these youngsters must have had an impish sense of humour. One Sunday we were unfortunately unable to locate an unexploded grenade. Obeying regulations, the Weapons Training Officer and Bombing Officer had the whole area wired off, and put up a notice, " DANGER— KEEP OUT—UNEXPLODED BOMB." Four days afterwards the W.T.O. had a plaintive telephone call from a Warden in a nearby district. Would he please come and look at an unexploded bomb in such-and-such a place ? Puzzled, the obliging W.T.O. met the Warden and was led down a residential road. At the end of the road an area was wired off, and a notice-board proclaimed " Danger— Keep Out—Unexploded Bomb." He recognised the board and wire. Youngsters had taken them away from our range and erected them in an inoffensive road, holding up everybody for four days.

More weapons were given to us—the Anti-Tank Two-pounder and the Anti-Tank Rifle. It seemed strange to have reached the stage when the glut of weapons was embarrassing. At least it proved that production was meeting requirements, and more.

Though it may never have been put officially on paper, it was stated verbally that G.S. battalions of the Home Guard were now looked upon as the equivalent of the second-line battalions of the last war. The authorities relied on them to provide the younger generation with the basic training before passing on to the regular forces. This was a compliment. It was also an extraordinarily inexpensive method of producing an army. If all the pounds saved to the country by the H.G. had been put end to end, they might have stretched twice round the world. A similar remark applies to the profusion of pamphlets issued.

THIRD ANNIVERSARY OF THE H.G.

To this parade in London, inspected by His Majesty, we sent a detachment and the Battalion Band. Both did us great credit. In fact, the reputation earned by our Band on this parade created a subsequent demand for their services by higher authority. It was amusing to remember that once upon a time Bands had been frowned on, and their existence unrecognised.

The Battalion itself held a parade in the Queen's Mead, companies giving demonstrations of various training activities, and marching past the Mayor of Bromley, who happened to be an officer in the Battalion.

Until now we had been relying on dispatch riders and telephones. Apart from the G.P.O. 'phones, we had slowly and stealthily laid private·wires all over Bromley. In .act, "B" Company had reached a stage where the members could go for a country walk in almost any direction, tap in on one of the numerous lines, and talk to a friend at will.

With the introduction of radio telephone sets we were indeed getting highly professional. These sets had a limited range, but being portable had unlimited possibilities. There were the mysteries of the phonetic alphabet to learn. Bad language spelt in this alphabet had a much more gracious and dignified sound. We picked up or tried to pick up the various technical details involving the use of these sets. We sat on hills, half a mile apart, and talked to each other. At last we had reached that happy stage when speed of passing information was literally almost as quick as lightning.

In earlier exercises the jam in communications had always been the Big Bad Wolf. By using a blend of R.T., G.P.O. telephones, private lines and D.Rs., Battalion H.Q. at last solved the problem of getting information in and out swiftly. As this is more or less bound up with the operational role of the Intelligence Section it seems appropriate here to describe what these dignified old gentlemen did when they came to Battalion H.Q. to take their share in an exercise. Various systems had been devised, amended, whittled down. Gradually the process of receiving information, dealing with it, and sending it out became smooth, quick, and automatic. In the beginning, the atmosphere of this department in action had savoured of a crazy newspaper office in an American film. It was nobody's fault. Everybody in the H.G. had been so impressed with the importance of sending information that it grew into a torrent, a deluge—most of it quite unimportant. We learned by experience. Thus the message-writer's hand grew less cramped, the battle-board keeper's feet less twinkling. An ecclesiastical calm prevailed.

BLITZ 1943-44

The resumption of night raiding by the Hun coincided with one of our platoon dinners. We felt they had deliberately and specifically selected this night with malice aforethought. One or two of the thuds were unpleasantly close to the dinner, but festivities continued, while half a mile away another platoon assisted the Police by patrolling damaged shops and preventing looting.

This was the forerunner of a series of raids which lasted throughout the winter. The Hun mixed a great number of phosphorus incendiaries with his bouquets, and although the damage was nothing to be compared with the 1940-41 blitz, these raids naturally had a nuisance value. From time to time detachments of the Battalion turned out to assist the Police and C.D. One member was killed and two were seriously injured, though not on duty at the time. Our comrades of the A.A., in conjunction with the earth-shaking " Z " batteries, combined to put up the biggest aerial barrrage in history. The noise was terrific. The skies sparkled with showers of rockets—a Brock's benefit night could bear no comparison. We began to argue that there was more danger from our own falling stuff than from the Hun. Queer things like fossilised drain pipes whizzed through the air. We had almost forgotten these familiar sights and sounds, although there had been one odd incident in the Spring, when a German plane, hit by our A.A. shells or a night fighter, zoomed down over the roof-tops about midnight to dump itself neatly in a cricket ground, much to the annoyance of " C " Company, who found themselves either guarding the aircraft on the Sunday morning or collecting basketfuls of bits.

Sunday always seemed to be the day for dramatic events. On a cloudy Sunday night a German plane travelling across Bromley in a south-westerly direction appeared to be hit. Almost at once reports came through from opposite points of the compass saying that several German airmen had been seen baling out over Hayes Common. Though the night was inky, the fact that these reports coincided made it seem worth while to turn out a platoon to search for the airmen. In the meanwhile strange stories came through to the Police Station. A German airman had been shot behind " The George." This story was checked up and found to be incorrect. The platoon at Hayes, who knew every blade of grass there, combed the darkness without result.

About 3 o'clock in the morning the Company Commander rang up to give a nil report. In the middle of his telephone conversation he said, dramatically, " Hullo ! I've just heard a rifle shot. There is something doing," and rang off. To the platoon waiting in the dark silence, the crack of a shot on the Common was electrifying. Some darted off in cars, followed by the rest on foot. Disenchantment met them. The shot had been fired by a car load of regular troops at some wandering tramp who had failed to stop when they challenged him. (No fun for tramps, this war.)

Dame Rumour had a glorious night. Not long after dawn the lordly ones were on the telephone, demanding a full report. They had learned from sources on which they had failed to check back that hordes of paratroops had been dropped in our area, and we had been fighting them all night. It seemed almost cruel to take all the glamour out of their excitement by telling them the extremely minor facts of the case.

COMPANY CLERKS.

Like St. Paul, the Company Clerk had to be all things to all men. It was a civilian appointment, authorised in a rather airy-fairy way by the War Office, who gaily stated that the employment of three clerks would relieve the Company Commander of all paper work.

In fact, the C.C. combined the duties of secretary, whipper-in of Returns, orderly room sergeant and carrier-of-the-can back when it involved a spot of paper bother with Battalion Head-quarters.

At Battalion Headquarters itself we had Miss J. Woodrow. From the beginning to the end she was with us, and her knowledge of H.G. administration and affairs in general proved invaluable. We also had J. Wright, who came straight from school to become the Filing King. Say to him : " About three years ago we had a letter asking for the number of dimpled Home Guards in Downham. Can you find it ? "—and still smiling, he would vanish among the tiers of files, and reappear like a flash with the wanted letter.

The following were with us during the dates stated :

Battalion Headquarters

Miss J. Woodrow	May 1940-Dec. 1944
Miss B. M. Sage	Oct. 1940-Jan. 1942
Miss M. Betts	Jan. 1942-Jan. 1943
Mrs. M. A. Burton	Jan. 1943-Oct. 1943
Mrs. E. G. Alchin	Oct. 1943-Dec. 1944
C. Storch	Nov. 1941-Aug. 1942
R. Ford	Aug. 1942-Oct. 1942
J. A. Wright.	Oct. 1942-Dec. 1944

A Company

Miss K. Bullen..	Nov. 1940-Nov. 1941

| Miss S. Young | Nov. 1941-July 1944 |
| Miss I. I. Knight | July 1944-Dec. 1944 |

C Company

| Mrs. P. M. Langdon .. | Jan. 1942-Dec. 1944 |

Mobile Column

| Miss Q. Rabley | June 1942-June 1943 ` |
| Mrs. D. Morris | .. June 1943-Sept. 1944 |

E Company

| Mrs. M. Kind (honorary) | Sept. 1942-Dec. 1944 |

WOMEN AUXILIARIES

Unofficially we had made use of ladies for H.G. purposes quite early in affairs. Under the directions of our M.O., they had taken lectures in First Aid and turned out on our exercises to man First Aid Posts (whether technically it is possible for a woman to man a post is a doubtful point). After a deal of consideration, the authorities decided that Battalions should be entitled to enrol a quota of Women Auxiliaries, to serve in various capacities such as Communications, Cooking, and First Aid. About 40 enrolled with us. They certainly did so without any desire for sartorial glamour, as the only official equipment issued to them was a badge. Later, for some startling and inexplicable reason, their title was changed to " Nominated Women." It says much for their forbearance that they took this without a murmur, or at any rate, without much of a murmur. Yet this minor murmur must have persisted with effect because presently their curious title was dropped.

SPORT AND PLEASURE

Cricket and football teams had been run by the companies for some time before we started to turn out a Battalion side. At cricket we did fairly well, and at football won the Sector Cup for the 1943-44 season, after a breathlessly exciting final, in which the spectators kicked more goals than the players. Most of the companies ran regular fixtures, and besides the two main sports, bowls was a popular sideline. As regards indoor entertainment there were dances galore, dinners and suppers, and during one season these latter were so numerous and the platoons so generous with their invitations that some of the H.Q. officers almost decided to board out on a bed-and-breakfast basis.

The Mess at Battalion H.Q. served as a popular meeting place for officers and also as an excellent room for lectures, at the end of which the audience invariably seemed as dry as the lecturer. We had no historic trophies to hang on the walls, but the Battalion flag, which was presented by the Sector Commander, lent the place the right touch and the collection of Battalion photographs grew and grew. The M.G. Company, having their H.Q. so close, were the most regular visitors—so regular that it was proposed to erect a plaque on the wall stating, "The officers of 51 K.H.G. M.G. Company lived here from 1942-44."

To bring people together in the Home Guard was one of the minor problems, the average member leading an existence rather limited by geography. Men in different company areas had had scanty opportunities of meeting each other, going up to their civil occupations from different stations, and never crossing each other's trails. By means of exercises and social affairs we managed to mix our personnel. We were lucky in not being one of those scattered battalions such as existed in very rural areas, where the average member of a platoon never saw his battalion commander.

PAPER

Troops in the Stone Age were to be envied. Presumably they could neither read nor write. There must have been times when many a Home Guard prayed for illiteracy. The paper spate was like an avalanche. Admittedly there are certain difficulties peculiar to the Home Guard. Whereas in a regular unit an Orderly Sergeant can call personnel together and give them instructions on the spot, in a H.G. battalion the only workable method is to pass information via the company commander to the platoon commander, thence to the section leader, thence to the members of the section. No easy task, particularly if members live far apart. A certain amount of paper was unavoidable, but it was felt that higher authority never appreciated the difficulties of the situation. Men were in the H.G. to carry out training, not to waste their time poring over paper. We felt that a good deal of the communications received from up above should never have been born. Like many members of the political, clerical and civil service worlds, the average Regular Army Officer is bad at one thing—short simple English. There was also a rather disturbing vagueness about the marking of documents with the word "Secret." One hush-hush envelope thus marked contained the following letter: "Every battalion is entitled to one bicycle for the use of the P.S.I."

1944

THE fourth winter of training loomed as a delicate matter. Everybody was getting a little war weary, a little older, a little less receptive at the end of a tiring day's civil work. The art of putting over instruction became all important. It had always been appreciated that an expert did not necessarily make a good instructor, and the old Army habit of teaching from the book had been discouraged. To make revision interesting was a problem. We arranged for each company and the Intelligence Section to work up a " show," this to combine instruction with entertainment and to be based on one particular aspect of training. Companies accepted the scheme with enthusiasm, selecting their casts and putting in a tremendous amount of work. Each Company gave its show to all the others, and during the early Spring we were able to boast of seven touring shows complete with scenery and props. Perhaps special mention should be made of " D " Company, who produced a number of transformation scenes to illustrate battle-craft. The Intelligence Section gave their final performance to an audience of the Police, C.D., W.V.S., etc., the theme being how not to run Battalion Battle H.Q., and then the right way to run it. The compere was careful to tell his audience that the wrong way of doing things was being put on first.

Some very vigorous exercises for officers were run in the early Summer, so vigorous, in fact, that some of them pleaded shortage of breath. On one of these a positive master stroke of tactics was performed. A small force of " enemy " landed at a certain point, and a larger Home force had to size up the situation, decide where the " enemy " were making for and take action. One of the "enemy", feeling rather out of breath, was given the peaceful job of slinking along to Home force H.Q. and throwing a bomb, just to make things more lively; but the Home force, thirsting to wipe out the " enemy," had all left their H.Q. and moved off. So the solitary " enemy" captured the empty H.Q. single-handed, and found peace in an armchair.

With the unguessable date of " D " Day approaching, we were given the highly interesting operational role of providing counter-attack forces should the Germans attempt to land paratroops to sabotage an important R.A.F. centre in our area.

Naturally we laid on various exercises to practise this operational role, and on one occasion an officers' platoon, assuming the role of paratroops, attacked the R.A.F. H.Q., which was protected by heavy barricades of dannert and barbed wire. One officer, risking at least damage to his trousers, managed to shin over the wire, elude the defences, and plant a symbolic bomb in the most vital spot. The Group Captain, watching affairs from the roof, popped his head over the edge and frankly announced, " You've won."

TASK PLATOON

In April it was obvious that " D " Day could not be so very far off. Judging that, when operations were opened on the Western front, the Germans might hit back with airborne raids, dropping small but highly trained bands to carry out sabotage, the authorities ordered battalions to put into operation the scheme known as the Task Platoon. This was to be a platoon ready for battle, mustered at night at a central H.Q., and ready to go out and fight at a moment's notice. The first platoon assumed the duty on April 29. This new responsibility meant extra hours of duty to most H.Gs., but they positively jumped at it. They felt that they were really doing something, taking a part in the forthcoming invasion. As each platoon took its turn on the rota, it prayed that that particular night the balloon might go up. They practised issuing ammunition, collecting their weapons, and turning out in the darkness. There is no doubt about it, if their services had been called on they would have been on the track of any paratroops in record time. Task Platoon Commanders considered the various possible eventualities and made plans adaptable to any specific situation. An atmosphere of war was in the air.

This Task Platoon duty continued until the end of August. It was arduous, in the sense that numbers of men found themselves booked either for this duty or a guard or picquet every eight or nine nights. Their only complaint was that enemy paratroops failed to materialise. For that we apologise.

FLYING BOMBS

A week after " D " Day, early in the morning, something that sounded like a plane diving at terrific speed passed overhead. The noise of its engines, sounding like some gigantic motor-cycle, was unusual. It was our first flying bomb. Within a day or two life had taken on a new and understandably apprehensive aspect. By day and by night this hideous secret weapon of Hitler came roaring over. A few miles to the south of us a balloon barrage spread and deepened. It was some comfort to see these balloons rising above the skyline. They grew to such a density that it seemed impossible that any flying bomb could get through. The A.A. guns which had started by firing on the doodle bugs as they passed overhead were moved down to the coast. Certainly the balloon barrage brought down its quota. We used to hear that distant familiar ugly droning and then a crash, and knew that another of those cables in the air had done its work. Despite these defences, twelve hundred flying bombs passed over the Bromley neighbourhood. Forty-one crashed in the Battalion area, and some two hundred within a radius of five miles of Battalion H.Q.

It began to be clear that the function of the Task Platoon was changed. The likelihood of dealing with paratroops lessened to vanishing point. Instead, it was obvious that they would be required to assist at flying bomb incidents. On several nights they were turned out to help the Police and C.D.

During the daylight hours we became builders, carpenters, tilers. Just under ten thousand houses in the borough were damaged. There was nowhere near enough civil labour available to cope with repairs. To make windows and roofs weatherproof became a matter of critical urgency. So every night platoons and companies got on with the work. Those who had never been on a roof before learned how to straddle rafters and fix tarpaulins. Hundreds of us became quite expert with wooden battens and " windolite " or sisal. The way the men turned out was magnificent. Those whose houses had been bombed and still required repairs would come along to patch up other people's houses. Many a time these repair parties were asked for at the shortest notice. When the area around Wharton Road Schools was damaged in the afternoon there were 150 men working full steam ahead there in the evening. By reason of practice and experience, we became highly organised in this new H.G. duty. On every site we had an Incident Officer, whose duty it was to survey the damage in conjunction with the C.D. Officer, to allot the tasks and detail the parties. A flying squad of tilers was trained. For a period the number of personnel engaged on these repairs was never less than 900 a week. Repair work took priority over training.

From the point of view of the Battalion, the motto was speed. Wherever possible we aimed at completing first aid repairs the same day as the incident occurred. This could not always be done, but on many occasions we started repairs on sites before the local authority could give any assistance. We helped the neighbouring

Borough of Beckenham, which suffered even more damage than Bromley, and reached the point where we were so loaded with repair work that there was not a single man left to spare. Numbers of sincerely appreciative letters were received from local residents, who showed their gratitude in various ways, the most amusing case being that of a dear old lady, obviously hard up, who offered one of our wealthiest platoon commanders five shillings.

We sent round " personal assistance " parties to help individual householders in any way they chose. All through this time there was the problem of bombed-out furniture. Our men did a lot of work in this direction, moving the furniture to various points and stacking it. Also there was the dirty and sometimes malodorous job of debris clearance. Dozens of roads in the borough were lined with piles of debris, plaster, glass, broken tiles and brickwork, the black and filthy dust that had accumulated under old roofs. These sights were most depressing, and it was felt that to clear them quickly would be a tonic to public morale. Local authority, snowed under by the number of incidents with which it had to cope, was unable to shift this debris. So we assumed responsibility for the job, delegating the clearance of the various areas to the companies concerned. Where the Borough could not supply sufficient transport we were authorised to hire. Shovels scraped and brooms swished. Besides being an eminently dirty job, it was also an eminently thirsty one. Arrangements were made for mobile canteens to visit the parties, but no steps were taken to advise personnel of the map references of the " locals," as this seemed unnecessary. The amount of debris shifted ran into hundreds of tons.

To deal with the job in a more wholesale fashion we once had high hopes of using a kind of glorified bulldozer. This actually arrived on the scene, but when the sapper in charge saw the debris he shook his head sadly and said, " No go." This 20-ton affair had been designed for bulldozing its way through smashed towns such as Caen, and he explained that if it were used for clearing our debris it would scoop this up all right, but it would also scoop up the pavement and the road. So we thanked him, and he took the giant home.

TRAINING

Possibly because of their advanced knowledge of the enemy's intentions regarding flying bombs and other forms of beastliness, it was decided that ten men per platoon should receive training in C.D. work, and that subsequently another ten per platoon should receive instruction from members of the first course. This training was most admirably put over by Civil Defence instructors, and as most of the personnel attending were selected on account of their practical knowledge, the result was a tremendous success. Besides being a change from ordinary H.G. training, the course had a solidly practical value. All the lectures were followed up with demonstrations, and the students were able to handle materials and actually carry out what they had seen illustrated on the blackboard. The most popular of the items (except for the victim concerned) was lowering a patient on a stretcher out of a high window. Subsequently, members of the Battalion volunteered to act as extra personnel at night at the various C.D. depots, ready to go out immediately to tackle any incidents. These C.D. instructors were fine, and earned our respect and admiration.

REVERSION TO VOLUNTARY BASIS

On September 6 Sir James Grigg gave his famous broadcast (famous at any rate from the H.G. point of view), and we realised that this was the prelude to the swan song. An end had to come sometime, though it was felt that the matter might have been handled in a different fashion. However, facts were facts. For a while we were to revert to a voluntary basis and then stand down. After four and a half years the thing seemed impossible. H.G. parades had become a part of our lives. What was the average man to do with his evenings and Sunday mornings?

Temporarily, until the actual Stand Down order was issued, we continued to hold parades, though these became more of a social nature, involving competitions and lectures on various subjects. Stand Down itself took effect from November 1, and after that remained the task of collecting in the very considerable quantity of arms, ammunition and equipment for return to the Home for Aged and Incurable Military Stores.

INSPECTION OF THE BATTALION BY LORD GORT, V.C.

Anticipating an actual farewell parade, an inspection of the Battalion by Lord Gort, V.C., was arranged to take place on the Queen's Mead, Bromley, on Sunday, September 17. For once the weather obliged. We were lucky to get the Field Marshal to inspect us, and this might not have been possible but for the fact that he happened to be a friend of our C.O. He came down, bringing as his A.D.C. his son-in-law, Major Philip Sidney, V.C., recently back from Italy, and Col. Leslie Graham, M.C., until recently Commander of our Sub-District.

After the General Salute had been given, Lord Gort inspected the Battalion in a most thorough manner, speaking to every third or fourth man and enquiring about his previous service. With the Band playing bravely, the sun brilliant, bayonets glinting, and the background of tall green trees, it was a spectacle most of us will always remember, and though officially it could not be called a farewell parade, we knew in our own hearts that this was the last time most of us would be gathered all together in ceremonial circumstance. In Lord Gort's address to us, he mentioned that it was the first time he had inspected a H.G. Battalion, and how much he had appreciated the opportunity to do so.

After the Field Marshal had taken the salute as the Battalion marched past, he joined the officers and their ladies at tea at Yeomanry House.

DINNER TO COMMANDING OFFICERS

Lt.-Cols. Etchells and O'Brien were invited as guests of honour to the dinner given by the Battalion Officers on September 29. It was a very happy affair. The second-in-command, Major H. D. Reynolds, M.C., in a short speech, pointed out how fortunate we had been in having two commanding officers of such outstanding ability. A little later, the two commanding officers also showed their versatility by singing *There is a tavern in the town*, Col. O'Brien accompanying on the piano.

THE END OF IT ALL

Evidently Higher Authority decided that the H.G. were old soldiers, for they arranged that we should fade away rather than die. October and November we spent handing in weapons and equipment. To be just, it must be admitted that a snappy end was technically impossible. But somehow we could not help remembering *The Mikado* and that memorable remark : " Let it be something linger-rr-ing."

Yes, it lingered. Yet it gave us the opportunity to start the foundation of a Battalion Old Comrades' Association, the future of which lies in the extending hands of Time.

On December 3, His Majesty broadcast a farewell message, and a detachment from the Battalion and the Band represented us on the farewell parade in London.

For four and a half years something unique in the military history of Britain had held its own, and now it was ended.

We were very, very sorry.

THE BATTALION BAND.

Taken at the final "Stand Down" Parade in Hyde Park, December 3, 1944.

Back Row: A. Nunn, W. Goodsell, F. Parisienne, E. Garlick, R. Hookway, C. Adnams, S. Wheeler, H. Garlick, H. W. Crampton, H. G. Crampton, E. Carpenter, C. Wright.

Centre Row: W. Anscombe, L./Cpl. E. Donnelly, B. Dunford, D. Mitchell, J. Randall, C. Butcher, A. Robjant, T. Coton, F. New, R. O'Dell, H. Putnam, S. Nash.

Front Row: J. Bowell, E. Harman, A. Peel, D. Grinstead, Sgt. G. Northfield, Capt. F. French (Quartermaster), Lieut. S. J. Craker (Bandmaster), Cpl. C. Singer, L./Cpl. W. Glen, A. Harrild, A. Smith.

SOME OF
THEM

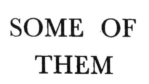

THE COMMANDING OFFICER'S
FINAL ADDRESS

Past and present members of the Battalion met at the Gaumont Cinema, Bromley, on November 26, 1944, when the Commanding Officer addressed them as follows :

When Field Marshal Lord Gort came to visit us in Bromley a few weeks ago and honoured us by inspecting the 51st Battalion and affiliated Units, we were not allowed at the time to refer to the occasion as being anything in the nature of a Stand Down Parade, and yet many of us, I am sure, had an idea that it was likely to be the last time we should be on parade as a Battalion, coming as it did, rather by judgment than by luck, so soon after the celebrated broadcast by the Secretary of State for War putting us back on a voluntary basis ; a broadcast, I might add, which caused considerable controversy and brought so much criticism, a good deal of which criticism, in my humble opinion, was both uncalled for and undignified.

When, however, the official Stand Down order came along, I decided that it would be unwise to attempt to hold another Battalion parade so soon afterwards. Bearing in mind how successful the previous one had been, I was anxious to avoid anything in the nature of an anti-climax, and preferred to keep the memory of that one as our final parade, but I must confess that I was disappointed that the chance of addressing the Battalion myself before we ceased to be a military unit seemed to have passed. Consequently, I seized the opportunity which this meeting offered, and it may well be that the comfort of a seat in the stalls may provide a more receptive audience than would have been the case if you were standing on parade in an English November.

But, now that I have the opportunity, what can I say ? I am sure you would not wish or expect me to thank you for doing your duty. Nor do I want to create the impression that this is in any way a farewell speech. Surely, none of us would wish to say good-

D   [45]

bye just when we have come to realise the value of so many new-found friends.

There is a great deal of difference between a man who just does what he has to do and the man who does that and some more. The difference cannot be measured by the amount of work done so much as by the spirit which prompts a man to do more than he is legally bound to do, and I have always believed that I have been more fortunate than many other Home Guard Battalion Commanders in having around me so many who have done a great deal more than could be legally demanded of them. They have done it because they realised that the success of the show depended upon it, and it was for that whole-hearted co-operation which so many of you have given that I shall be eternally thankful. I cannot omit from my thanks the hundreds of mothers, wives, and sweethearts who, by their magnificent, unselfish courage, often during long periods of anxiety and danger, had made it possible for you to give of your best.

There is no doubt, Gentlemen, that the Home Guard can look back on a fine job of work well done, but may I here offer a word of warning. From the exaggerated claims being made by some who think they are doing the Home Guard a service, one would imagine that, in spite of the Civil Defence Services, the Regular Forces and hosts of other unsung heroes, the Home Guard had won the war. Let us not lose our sense of proportion. Undoubtedly, the Home Guard has played an important role in the main strategic plan which has made possible the great victories which we and our Allies have won during the recent months, but the war is not yet won, and it would be as well to remember that, while we are standing easy, our brothers in the Regular Forces are fighting, and will yet have to fight battles of unprecedented fury before final victory is ours.

There is so much that we can do to help. Need I remind you of the warning given by the Prime Minister as recently as November 9 last at the Mansion House, when he was being entertained by the Lord Mayor of London, whom we are proud to honour as a member of the 51st Battalion. Mr. Churchill said then : " No one can be blamed, provided he does not slacken his or her efforts for a moment—no one can be blamed for hoping that victory may come to the Allies and peace to Europe in 1945." That does not mean that the victory will come to us easily, and the words are those of one who, by his own courage and hard work has indeed earned for himself the right to demand our attention.

And there is one other way in which we can contribute so much.

We can do all in our power to keep alive that spirit of comradeship which has been the lifeblood of the Home Guard. It was something priceless. In doing so we can have the satisfaction of knowing that at the same time we are helping to lay the foundations of a real peace, for we shall surely need that comradeship in the years to come as much as we have needed it and learnt its value in the terrible years of war.

I wish you all the very best of luck and I look forward to many years in which I can recall with you so many instances of how happiness can be born from adversity.

THE HYDE PARK PARADE

The following represented the Battalion at the Hyde Park Parade on December 3, 1944, when H.M. The King took the salute :

1149 Lieut. C. A. Monks	C Company
469 Lieut. F. Downing	M.G. Company
896 Lieut. E. D. Walpole	E Company
2560 L.-Cpl. S. C. Kent	A Company
804 Pte. C. Connew	
905 Pte. E. Jennison	,,
853 Cpl. J. H. Brown	B Company
217 Pte. H. A. Smart	
2282 Pte. J. A. F. Tomkins	,,
831 Cpl. E. Cowdrey	C Company
148 Pte. A. Reynolds	
65 Pte. R. A. Podger	,,
2006 Cpl. F. P. Maddison	D Company
2589 Cpl. S. C. Cox	
1369 L.-Cpl. Barker	
1024 Pte. E. Goodger	
2728 Pte. W. Armstrong	,,
2150 Cpl. S. G. Crittenden	Mobile Column
2235 Pte. F. E. Cutler	,, ,,
549 Pte. J. C. Wingrove	,, ,,
2185 Cpl. D. S. Hurley	M.G. Company
2677 L.-Cpl. S. Badis ..	
1272 L.-Cpl. H. J. Leonard	,,
1231 Pte. E. V. Hanon	,,\
2942 Pte. E. J. Humphrey ..	,,

and
The Battalion Band

HONOURS & AWARDS

M.B.E. (Military Division)
No. 90 Volunteer S. W. ANTHONY, D Company.
No. 633 Volunteer W. E. WHYBROW, A Company.

London Gazette, 22-1-41

CERTIFICATES FOR GOOD SERVICE

New Year's Honours, 1942
No. 275 Corporal C. G. POWELL, D Company.

The King's Birthday Honours, 1942
No. 400 Sergeant S. F. BAGSHAW, Headquarters.

New Year's Honours, 1943
No. 361 Company-Sergeant-Major H. JENNER, M.G. Company.

The King's Birthday Honours, 1943
Captain F. D. HOYS, Adjutant.
No. 604 Sergeant H. J. STARR, B Company.
No. 575 Corporal J. L. WHITE, A Company.

New Year's Honours, 1944
No. 73 Sergeant H. THOMSON, C Company.

The King's Birthday Honours, 1944
No. 849 Colour-Sergeant W. B. MORAN, E Company.
No. 2209 Lance-Corporal T. W. HOILES, Signals.

New Year's Honours, 1945
No. 173 Sergeant A. J. HUMPHREY, Band.
No. ED21 Sergeant H. E. ARMSTRONG, Electricity Unit.
No. 3 Corporal C. H. ROLLSTON, Intelligence Section.
No. 1901 Corporal F. C. CARTER, Heavy Transport Section.
No. 39 Lance-Corporal J. A. HYDEN, Mobile Column.

Nominal Roll of the Battalion
May 1940 — September 1944

No.	Name	No.	Name	No.	Name
May, 1940.		50	Wattenbach, C. V.	101	Sutton, F.
1	Hulk, F. W. L.	51	Kirton, J.	102	Harvey, E. W. S.
2	Jeffs, G. R.	52	Kinghorn, W. H.	103	Squibb, E. J.
3	Rollston, C. R.	53	Harris, H. L.	104	Lewis, R. I.
4	Lewis, J. C.	54	Weston, A.	105	Byford, A. G.
5	Harrild, W. L.	55	Burford, A. E.	106	Thomson,
6	Pocock, G. A.	56	Langham, A. E.		W. G. H.
7	Hoys, F. D.	57	Craker, P. W.	107	Wimble, A. S.
8	O'Brien, H. W.	58	Forrester, M. W	108	Oxenham, J. B.
9	Jorgensen, J. R. C.	59	Heath, F.	109	Vickers, J.
10	Tosland, H. A.	60	Etchells, T.	110	Bowman, F.
10A	Lane, E.	61	Warner, A. E.	111	Timms, W. H.
11	Armstrong, G. S.	62	Ryan, D. P.	112	Price, R. A.
12	Himus, G. W.	63	Aylott, J.	113	Brodrick, G. W.
12A	Harris, F. L.	64	Boyd, G. M.	114	Merritt, A. T.
13	Loder, A. S.	65	Podger, R. A.	115	Johnston, J.
14	Shepherd, P. C.	66	Osman, J. H.	116	Walpole, W. G.
15	Allen, R. N.	67	Wright, A. W.	117	Bush, L. P.
16	Webster, A. N. S.	68	Forrester, E.	118	Davey, T. A.
17	Clarke, W. H.	69	Comins, C. J.	119	Webster, F. K.
18	Perrett, H. F.	70	Prebble, S.	120	Spearman, F. T.
19	Ivey, G. W. L.	71	Beaumont, S. G.	121	Mills, A.
20	Hansen, A. E.	72	Allen, C. E.	122	Mitchell, A.
21	Killick, E. J.	73	Thomson, H.	123	Gale, E. H.
22	Devereux, E.	74	Shears, R. S.	124	Merrill, J.
23	Coleman, H.	75	Hotter, A. N.	125	Gebbett, F. G.
24	Hancock, A. G.	76	Brown, P. G.	126	Phillips, A. B.
25	Wall, E. A.	77	Suter, E.	127	Tottem, F. A.
26	Brice, E. G.	78	Collins, E. H.	128	Elwood, W. T.
27	Block, H. W.	79	Attenborough,	129	Dickinson, J. H. A
28	Rand, V. T.		E. R. S.	130	Butler, W. G.
29	Elliott, L. J.	80	Green, G. A.	131	Powell, L. C.
30	King, F. B.	81	Perry, F. H.	132	Ironside, W.
31	Cheshire, C. A.	82	Johnson, S. W.	133	Jeffery, W. J.
32	Wills, J. H. F.	83	Lefeaux, W.	134	Avent, S. F.
33	Davies, W. E.	84	Thomsett, W. L.	135	Mack, J. D.
34	Cox, A. I.	85	Smith, A. J.	136	Gooch, H. R.
35	Vokins, F.	86	Sutton, R. J.	137	Lake, J. S.
36	Grant, T. C.	87	Rogers, R. B.	138	Ross, E. S.
37	Young, H. E. V.	88	Robinson, L. H. A	139	Shine, G. W.
38	Brown, I. M. W.	89	Perry, A. A.	140	Stanger, F. J.
39	Hyden, J. A.	90	Anthony, S. W.	141	Dungate, J. H.
40	Beech, H.	91	Brunner, J. T.	142	Hale, P.
41	Hartridge, E. N.	92	Bark, F. J.	143	Wratton, W. G.
42	Dowley, S. E.	93	Matthias, O. G.	144	Targett, J. J.
43	Rose, S. H. C.	94	Lake, D. H. C	145	Briggs, T. W.
44	Pallett, J. W.	95	Wade, R.	146	Swift, R. A.
45	Bowell, J. H.	96	Price, J. A.	147	Hay, L. H.
46	Wood, H. S.	97	Andrews, R. C.	148	Reynolds, A.
47	Timms, H. A	98	Butcher, F. J.	149	Hufton, F. C.
48	Pickering, A. H.	99	Mason, V. F. B.	150	Towers, P. M.
49	Scotcher, T. B.	100	Harbar, A. H.	151	Stent, G. H. S.

No.	Name	No.	Name	No.	Name
152	Shergold, E. W.	209	Puplett, E. C.	266	Dennis, C.
153	Brooker, J.	210	Tilling, H. W.	267	Hayles, C. R.
154	Crossman, C. A. F.	211	Poulter, S.	268	Wallace, T. C. J.
155	Troquet, P.	212	O'Neill, H.	269	Brodie, R.
156	Brown, L. S.	213	Cattley, E.	270	Stockwell, F.
157	Clark, H. V.	214	Grimani, L. E.	271	Soar, E. D.
158	Waters, A. H.	215	Gleason, A. J. G.	272	Timms, S. W.
159	Lovett, J.	216	Lewis, E. W.	273	Garcia, C. F.
160	Hodgkin, A. A.	217	Smart, H. A.	274	Jolliffe, C. C.
161	Owen, F. R.	218	Tidbury, F.	275	Powell, C. G.
162	Clark, P. W.	219	Campbell, K. C.	276	Taylor, E. F.
163	Williams, E. F.	220	Langridge, F. E.	277	Rimmer, M. C.
164	Holroyde, F. J.	221	Elliott, G. H.	278	Dunn, D. R.
165	Strachan, G. L.	222	Travis, C. G.	279	Goodall, A. G.
166	Waite, J. J.	223	Ryley, A. N.	280	Southgate, E. A
167	Chandler, H.	224	Russell, A.	281	Roberts, J. W.
168	Sayer, B. T.	225	Pattison, R. W.	282	Bullen, T. A.
169	Hodges, F. E.	226	Sandford, H.	283	Wager, F.
170	Smith, W. D.	227	Martina, E. L.	284	Watts, A.
171	Barnard, C. ·	228	Wenham, F.	285	Atkins, W. J.
172	Ballard, W. A. S.	229	Carrie, D. J.	286	Smith, S. B.
		230	Brand, H. G.	287	Clarke, H. S.
June, 1940.		231	Masters, H. J.	288	Cleeves, J. W.
173	Humphrey, A. J.	232	Varcoe, W. A.	289	Sergeant, H. L.
174	Harper, C. F.	233	Hanna, C. H.	290	Ellis, J. H. E.
175	Bloxham, H.	234	Shenton, G. J.	291	Williams, J. R.
176	Flanders, G. M.	235	Garman, F.	292	Stedman, P. G.
177	Bilham, S. W.	236	Eaglestone, H.	293	Weeks, A. E.
178	Butler, P. F.	237	Firminger, L. D.	294	Culyer, A. L.
179	Heppel, J. B.	238	Willison, C. W.	295	Hurrell, A.
180	Startup, F.	239	Wood, F. H.	296	Standfield, J. H.
181	Smith, P. W.	240	Riordan, J. L.	297	Hopkin, H. L.
182	Coombes, F. G. S.	241	Cowling, N. L.	298	Gledhill, R. S.
183	Judd, F. W.	242	Warwick, W. J.	299	Smith, H. B.
184	Parker, R.	243	Lunn, L. C.	300	Broughton,
185	Woodroffe, G. E.	244	Clark, A.		B. H. E.
186	Caswell, F. W.	245	Morris, W. J.	301	Ingman, F. R.
187	Harris, F. G.	246	Buttle, E. F. E.	302	Taylor, H. W.
188	Johnson, W. C.	247	Wise, F.	303	Prior, W.
189	Jennings, S. J.	248	Armson, G. A.	304	Driskell, F. G.
190	Bridgeland, J.	249	McLaren, D.	305	Wells, A. G.
191	Cook, P. M.	250	New, L. C. T.	306	Darby, J. B.
192	Hayes, L.	251	Hollingsworth,	307	Weekes, R. W.
193	Funnell, V. J.		A. C.	308	Morgan, H. E.
194	Hogg, D.	252	Higgins, L. B.	309	Billings, C. H. L.
195	Cooper, L. N. H.	253	Clark, R. J.	310	Christie, G. C.
196	Thomas, W.	254	Saunders, H. E. D.	311	Taylor, J. A.
197	Holland, S. J.	255	Lock, G.	312	Heal, A. V.
198	Warran, W. S.	256	Hodder-Williams,	313	Carlyon, C. J.
199	Thompson, F. G.		R. P.	314	Sedler, E. J.
200	Marshall, A. E.	257	Clothier, H. A.	315	Moxley, H. A.
201	Marshall, P. C.	258	Meades, E. G.	316	Pulley, A. S.
202	Arnold, C. L.	259	Gedge, E. G. D.	317	Ashler, F. P.
203	Price, R. J.	260	Nil	318	Summer, H. A.
204	Smith, H. E.	261	McLeod, A. R.	319	Brimacombe,
205	Drewett, W. E.	262	Whittle, H. A.		G. W.
206	Wood, S. B.	263	Horne, A. A.	320	Bebbington, H. J.
207	Hancock, F. S.	264	Raine, J.	321	Dixon, J. W.
208	Walker, M.C.	265	Hoyle, F. C.	322	Filby, A. E.

No.	Name	No.	Name	No.	Name
323	Thompson, A. W.	382	Mountfort, L. T. W.	440	Spicer, F. C.
324	Phillips, W. B.			441	Chard, J. J.
325	Bagnall, T.	383	Stephenson, H. D.	442	Bryant, F.
326	Fentiman, J.	384	Mackay, D.	443	Grunsell, A.
327	Butcher, C. B.	385	Chesson, G. C.	444	Wilmer, W. J. C.
328	Kerr, J. R.	386	Hodgson, H. C.	445	Wild, W. B.
329	Williams, H. J.	387	Youdell, C. J.	446	Haughton, C.
330	White, H. E.	388	Watson, W.	447	Williams, B.
331	Pocock, H.	389	Sanderson, T. W.	448	Trodd, L. T.
332	Birch, A. A.	390	Parkinson, H. F.	449	Smith, W. S.
333	Fairney, E. V.	391	Bligh, R. C.	450	Thatcher, P. A.
334	Lewis, E. R.	392	Brady, A. J.	451	White, A. W. V.
335	Denby, F.	393	Day, J.	452	Johnson, F. E.
336	Williams, J. H.	394	Green, W. J.	453	Fodew, T. R.
337	Hyde, H. A.	395	Walter, H. W.	454	Woodhams, E. J.
338	Mooves, J. J.	396	Knowles, E. G.	455	Winckle, D. P. S.
339	Ford, F.	397	Bissmire, H. S.	456	Morris, E. L.
340	Sykes, W. G. S.	398	Ives, F. H.	457	Lane, T.
341	Griffiths, A. E.	399	Butler, F. H. C.	458	Shorting, W. L.
342	Brooke, D.	400	Bagshaw, S. F.	459	Kinnear, A.
343	Hooker, F. L.	401	Marshall, T. W.	460	Ranson, E.
344	Tennant, W. C.	402	Barrow, S. C.	461	Weatherall, A. H.
345	Gomme, S. J.	403	Payne, H. H.	462	Carter, A. F.
346	Dean, A. D.	404	Taylor, C. D.	463	Shepperd, D. G.
347	Philip, H. C.	405	Reeves, F. H.	464	Smith, F. J.
348	Miller, A. W.	406	Cooke, G. S.	465	Everest, A. E.
349.	McDonald, J. W.	407	Cooper, C. H.	466	Ayers, P. S.
350	Dewsbury, R. B.	408	Driscoll, R. E.	467	Williamson, G. E.
351	Bullen, R. E.	409	Edser, H. A.	468	King, C. H.
352	Creamer, W. L.	410	Boyd, G. M.	469	Downing, F.
353	Mitchell, W. J.	411	Gurden, A. J.	470	Duncan, P.
354	Chinn, A. E.	412	Jamblin, C. R.	471	Menpes, C.
355	Bolton, H. W.	414	Leach, W. A.	472	Best, W. C.
356	Furley, K. G.	415	Lothian, F. J.	473	Thayre, A.
357	Guest, H. J.	416	Stanton, H.	474	Fitch, F. S.
358	East, J. W. N.	417	Mutimer, L.	475	White, P. C.
359	Sansom, F. J.	418	Coombes, F. J.	476	Ponsford, R. S.
360	Lansbury, R. G.	419	Arnaud, J. N.	477	Fawkner, H. S.
361	Jenner, H.	420	Turpin, H. T.	478	Townsend, E.
362	Cole, C. F.	421	Johnson, F. C.	478A	Duncan, P.
363	Woods, A. G.	422	Power, L. J. B.	479	Winch, J. M.
364	Goodman, R. G.	423	Rogers, C. A.	480	Lee, G. H.
365	Murrells, W. G.	424	Seager, W. G.	481	Holliday, C. A.
366	Heaysman, V. H.	425	Pepper, T. L. M.	482	Cope, S.
367	Ramsay, A.	426	Davis, T. H.	483	Tipshall, H.
368	Carter, L. J.	427	Sheppard, C. V.	484	Reynolds, L. J.
369	Packe, W. V.	428	Eke, F.	485	Bridgland, H. W.
370	Slark, E. H. E.	429	Easton, J. V. W.	486	Harris, G. H.
371	Neesham, C. V.	430	Waters Fuller, C. P.	487	Foulger, J. H.
372	Scott, R.	431	Handscomb, H. B.	488	Cave, W. T.
373	Dorsett, G. H.	432	Mynott, T. C.	489	Beer, C. M.
374	Nil	433	Collett, T. K.	490	Mason, A. G. E.
375	Goodhill, H. G.	434	Barrett, D. J.	491	Clarke, S. B.
376	Atkinson, T.	435	Littlewood, A.	492	Staples, H.
377	Marsh, W. R.	436	Hewens, C. J.	493	Jones, T. W.
378	.Harrod, G.	437	Sandle, S. E.	494	Johnson, F. W.
379	Boxshall, C. C. W.	438	Allan, J. J.	495	Norris, W. A.
380	Tiller, W.	439	Powell, E. A.	496	Reeve, R. W.
381	Short, H. E.			497	Clifton, C.

No.	Name	No.	Name	No.	Name
c498	Blake, G.	553	Kitchener, J. J. W.	612	Kitton, M. E.
499	Fullagar, C.	554	Morris, C. E.	613	Gurden, W. J.
500	Bedson, F. J.	555	Constable, G.	614	Hammond, E. E.
501	Beech, W. E.	556	Matthews, E. H. G	615	Fox, R. J.
502	Stevens, W.	557	Macfarlane, G. G.	616	Scofield, C. B.
503	Lane, T.	558	James, W. A.	617	Warwick, F.
504	Whittaker, H.	559	Rumball, H. C.	618	Campbell, E. D.
505	Meaden, D. G.	560	Osborn, B. W.	619	Clegg, G. R.
506	Dunn, E.	561	Cooke, D. G.	620	Trower, H.
507	Smethurst, H.	562	Cowburn, K. J.	621	Wright, B. W.
508	Johns, N. A.	563	Beamish, H. F.	622	Dibden, E. H.
509	Eyre, C. F.	564	Atha, H. M. G.	623	King, H.
510	Gruby, D. M.	565	Ostler, W. E.	624	Snelgrove, G. F.
511	Marmon, G. H. F	566	Newman, A. J.	625	Follett, J. P.
512	Whybrow, D. P.	567	Jenkins, A. H.	626	Warner, A. W.
513	Bowman, D.	568	Farris, R W.	627	Windsor, G. T. M.
514	Ford, G. E.	569	Reed, M.	628	Hammond, W.
515	Clarke, W. R.	570	Mason, D.	629	Payne, H. G.
516	Chalk, R. F.	571	Ball, F. F.	630	Whittaker, W. C.
517	Easton, D. H.	572	Menter, E.	631	Burleigh, H. B.
518	Garcia, R. A.	573	Brander, W. B. C.	632	Rand, J. J.
519	Hume, D. R.	574	Pettit, E. H.	633	Whybrow, W. L.
520	Thomson, L. W.	575	White, J. L.	634	Anderson, R. J.
521	Goodwin, F. J. D.	576	Ireland, G. F.	635	Pope, W. S.
522	Stemp, R.	577	Brockman, F. G.	636	Webb, W. S.
523	Reed, A. H.	578	Smith, R. C	637	Hunter, J. A.
524	Hammond, A. W.	579	Wallace, T. E. J.	638	Pigott, A, F.
525	Smithard, H. D.	580	Roberts, A. J.	639	Horsford, P.
526	Reynolds, H. D.	581	Treadwell, T.	640	Monks, C. M.
527	Wigley, P.	582	Bullen, W. H.	641	Evans, W. A.
528	Joyce, R. W.	583	Buckley, W.	642	Pallenden, P. G.
529	Wallis, E. C.	584	Silk, H. T.	643	Atha, L.
530	Hawkins, R. C.	585	James, F. C.	644	Jolly, W. R.
		586	Nil	645	Jeffree, F. W.
July, 1940.		587	Trehearne, A. J.	646	Smith, H. G.
531	Holland, R. J.	588	Carruthers, O.	647	Judd, F. V.
532	Hammond, G. A.	589	Diggins, J. C.	648	Badder, G. S.
533	Baldwin, F.	590	Coombe, L. D.	649	Waight, W. C. S.
534	Taylor, F.	591	McCree, W. B.	650	Roe, J. J. T.
535	Hose, A. S.	592	Brown, W.	651	Lyddiard, W. T.
536	Featherstone, A. E.	593	Robinson, S.	652	Cossins, C. G.
		594	Keyse, C. G. H.	653	Boulton, W. U.
537	Young, E. A.	595	Hill, H. R.	654	Price, T. J.
538	Barnard, P. J.	596	Champion, E. F.	655	Vink, H. K.
539	Lendon, E. C.	597	Killick, R.	656	Collett, J. C.
540	Finnimore, G.	598	Bradley, P.	657	Jones, W. J. P.
541	Barton, F. J.	599	Wickenden, B. S.	658	Wright, W. G.
542	Gothard, R.	600	Holland, J. W.	659	Butcher, C. F.
543	Wickham, J.	601	Wyatt, W. H.	660	Langley, C. J.
544	Nil	602	Harrison, E. G.	661	O'Hara, B. L.
545	Christopherson, G. R.	603	King, W. G.	662	Scott, W.
		604	Starr, H. J.	663	Crouch, F. W.
546	Kemp, A.	605	Boseley, C. J. J.	664	Bolton, W. F.
547	Clark, P. G.	606	Bishop, J. R.	665	Riley, R. F.
548	Mothers, R.	607	Davis, B. J. C.	666	Forsdick, J. A.
549	Wingrove, J. C.	608	Bishop, H. R.	667	Young, L. W. B.
550	Halsted, W. C. N.	609	Wallace, G. S.	668	Hunt, J. S. M.
551	Doggett, R.	610	Warwick, R. T.	669	Edwards, W. E.
552	Brockwell, P. S.	611	Chaffe, W. T.	670	Seed, L. G.

No.	Name	No.	Name	No.	Name
671	Tooke, D. F.	729	Paine, B. G.	786	Morris, G. F.
672	Easterby, H. W.	730	Smith, G. S.	787	Clarke, C. E.
673	Filmer, C. J.	731	Dwyer, P. J.	788	Benn, E.
674	Jones, E.	732	Janes, S. L. R.	789	Collins, C. W.
675	Stanley, W. R.	733	Beadle, J. A.	790	Saunders, M. G.
676	Fleming, H. B.	734	Chasty, E.	791	Oulton, J. H.
677	Budger, G. H.	735	Page, C. H.	792	Aldcroft, L.
678	Todd, T. S.	736	Towell, A. C.	793	Meaden, D. G.
679	Leather, V. S.	737	Garwood, H. R.	794	Mortimore, R. A.
680	Froud, A. G.	738	Moutrie, L.	795	Davies, D. T.
681	Harper, R. A	739	Davey, A.	796	Ford, B. R.
682	Everest, R. E.	740	White, J. F. T.	797	Paddon, A.
683	Campbell, I. C.	741	Drewitt, W. F.	798	Coomber, A. J.
684	Pearce, W. A.	742	Downs, G. W. F.	799	Batten, A. E.
685	Catmur, R. E.	743	Gordon, F. W.	800	Rackham, L. A.
686	Stopford, A.	744	Hawkes, N. A.	801	Walker, H. E.
687	Butte, F. J.	745	Parsons, E. H.	802	Parfett, D.
688	Ferris, L. J.	746	Barrett, P. J.	803	Franklin, J.
689	Burrowes, H. A.	747	Maskrey, L. W.	804	Connew, C.
690	Notman, F. C.	748	Hovey, W. J.	805	Holland, R. J.
691	Lindo, J. E.	749	Floyd, P. M.	806	Couper, J. A. V.
692	Hayles, S. G.	750	Blackwell, F. L.	807	Mitchell, A. B.
693	Windebank,	751	Moss, H. C.	808	Aldcroft, K. D.
	H. W. C.	752	Pallett, L. G.	809	Everton, R. E.
694	Kiddell, J. E. B.	753	Watson, S. J.	810	Willey, R. E.
695	Brown, W. A.	754	Anderson, F. G.	811	Seager, J. P.
696	Pepper, E. R.	755	Evans, G. T.	812	Hartman, T. B.
697	Hoblyn, H. B.	756	Bass, B. W.	813	Mills, E. M.
698	Whitaker, F.			814	Campbell,
699	Harrild, J. V.	**August, 1940.**			J. N. McK.
700	Armstrong, J. L.	757	Higgs, R. A.	815	Croucher, B. R.
701	Barton, F. R. C.	758	Parker, E. P.	816	Cox, H. J.
702	Pittar, W. J.	759	Harding, J.	817	Duke, W. H.
703	Wall, H. O.	760	Dorning, J. R. K.	818	Bone, J.
704	Spurdens, H.	761	Wood, R. E.	819	Penman, W. A.
705	Moore, C. H. G.	762	Smith, T. H.	820	Wise, G. G.
706	Whiteley, R. G.	763	Barnes, J. T.	821	Allen, H. C.
707	Reading, P. G.	764	Gorton, J. F.	822	Hamblin, G. R.
708	Hall, P.	765	Knapp, B. B.	823	Leader, W.
709	Sargent, A. R.	766	Luzmore, T.	824	Mitchell, E. F.
710	Bruce, H. P.	767	Emes, L. D.	825	Morgan, W. J.
711	Potts, R.	768	Windsor, H. A. L.	826	Stevens, A. J.
712	Googe, S. B.	769	MacHale, L. A.	827	Mansell, G. E.
713	Carter, P. D.	770	Norton, P.	828	Cooke, F. T.
714	Levey, G. A.	771	Parish, J. A.	829	Glock, W. H.
715	Ford, L. K.	772	East, G. P.	830	Macvie-Hill, C. G.
716	Lee, G. H., Jr.	773	Cashmore, T. L.	831	Cowdery, E.
717	Potts, D.	774	King, T.	832	Bridges, A. R.
718	Ketlow, F.	775	Rowbotham, R. R	833	Blackburn, C. H.
719	Tooke, H. E.	776	Ford, B. R.	834	Slade, E. J.
720	Marsh, F. R.	777	Webber, P. R.	835	Marriott, A. J.
721	Eyles, G. L.	778	Kinniburgh, W. J.	836	Smith, D. F.
722	Gamm, K. B.	779	Barber, J.	837	Hyde, C. W.
723	Fabry, J. T.	780	Dobbs, L. S.	838	Dangerfield, C. C
724	Harvey, K. T.	781	Hutchins, C. T.	839	Connor, L. R.
725	Parker, S. E.	782	Ashby, M.	840	Brook, R. N. R.
726	Gale, G. A.	783	Tykes, T. R.	841	Shaw, J.
727	Harris, J. L. A.	784	Carr, D. G.	842	Lane, F.
728	Hollick, F.	785	Sayers, J.	843	Dixon, G. E. B.

No.	Name	No.	Name	No.	Name
844	Tabor, O. H.	903	Newbury, W. H.	958	Harding, S. W.
845	Hall, S. W.	904	Kemp, J. A.	959	King, W. J.
846	Higson, A. C.	905	Jennison, E.	960	Storey, P. F.
847	Kennedy, G. W.	906	Oram, G. L.	961	Dabner, K. C.
848	Barratt, R. E.	907	Marston, L. W.	962	Love, C. B.
849	Moran, W. B.			963	Leborse, F. M.
850	Tibbles, J. C.	**September, 1940.**		964	Ware, K. A.
851	Holloway, W. R.	908	Smith, R. O.	965	Seal, J. D.
852	Gray, G. R.	909	Horsfall, C. D.	966	Newman, J. J.
853	Brown, J. H.	910	Hill, W. A. E.	967	Huard, C. P.
854	Stephenson, E. L.	911	Williams, H.	968	Williams, G.
855	Knight, W.	912	Henson, R. J.	969	Andrews, D. J. T.
856	Seabrooke, S. H.	913	Lewis, J. C.	970	Oliver, R. C.
857	Allchorn, F. W.	914	Prior, J. C.	971	Caird, G. O.
858	Thatcher, E. H.	915	Stevens, D. F.	972	Smith, F. W. W.
859	Nil	916	Foxton, D. F.	973	Hobbs, N.
860	Harding, W.	917	Penman, V. R.	974	Downey, T. R.
861	Muirhead, J.	918	Wernor, L. H. C.	975	Hamblin, M. D.
862	Goodway, H. F.	919	Mann, J. M.	976	Cardus, F.
863	Pettit, H. A.	920	Keall, G. E.	977	Tanner, D. E.
864	Pritchitt, F. W.	921	Gray, D. R.	978	Wellham, S. F.
865	Sugarman, R.	922	Henley, G. E.	979	Storey, B. R.
866	Cruttenden, H. S.	923	Bee, A. A.	980	Hainsworth, E. C.
867	Wright, W.	924	Arnold, A. W.	981	Coe, H. T.
868	Sayes, J. E. A.	925	Everitt, G. T.	982	Baker, S. A. C.
869	Hewitt, D. C.	926	Sayers, L. R.	983	Watson, J. T.
870	Moore, A. E.	927	Stiff, R. J.	984	Felby, G. A.
871	Hale, B. P.	928	Noonan, S.	985	Harper, F. E. W.
872	Robertson, W. H.	929	Dawson, D. S.	986	Stickland, D. R.
873	Hyde, J. A.	930	Waller, E. A.	987	Parissien, R. W.
874	Burton, B. C.	931	Burgess-Smith, K.	988	Olivo, A.
875	Waters, L. J.	932	Morgan, R. H.	989	Hall, D. H.
876	Pettit, G. F.	933	Gothard, C. F. S.	990	Woodward, T. J.
877	Halliday, D.	934	Rowe, L. J.	991	Portlock, G. F.
878	Knight, J. C.	935	Platt, I. G.	992	Hill, W. A.
879	Houston, J. W.	936	Hoskin, E. H.	993	Haine, W.
880	Mayhew, D. J.	937	Austin, A. E.	994	Nil
881	Hull, R. S.	938	Allain, J. E.	995	Bacon, C. E.
882	Shine, J. J.	939	Reeves, R. E.	996	Mitchell, D.
883	Wiltshire, D.	940	Phillips, F. B.	997	Moreton, C. H.
884	Deighton, H. J.	941	Laudais, G.	998	Wickenden, P. R.
885	Lines, W. J.	942	Groves, J. A.	999	Pilkington, P.
886	Kenny, E. P.	943	Withers, F. W. D.	1000	Peggs, J. E.
887	Robertson, J. P.	944	Burills, M. R.	1001	Ovens, S. A.
888	Phillips, G. D.	945	Gregory, C. D.	1002	Freeman, J. W.
889	Sutton, A. R.	946	Tarry, S. G.	1003	King, R. B. G.
890	Roberts, A. R.	947	Kimber, K. G.	1004	Johnston, W. A.
891	Judge, C. R. W.	948	Gillard, E. A.	1005	Lansbury, E. R.
892	Geere, C. E.			1006	Green, S. J.
893	Fowler, H. W.	**October, 1940.**		1007	Starkip, F. G.
894	Stockwell, A. J.	949	Levander, H. J.	1008	Cook, P. V.
895	Penfold, H. G.	950	Pickard, C. C.	1009	Savage, J. A
896	Walpole, E. D.	951	White, R. A.	1010	Freakes, R. A. M.
897	Clay, E. A.	952	Markin, E. T.	1011	Tidswell, V. E.
898	Drake, W. R.	953	Ball, R. J.	1012	Pratten, D. F.
899	Giles, E.	954	Constant, K. L.	1013	Payne, R. G. P.
900	Armstrong, N. E.	955	Whitehouse, D. F.	1014	Fenge, H. G. A.
901	Batchelor, F. C.	956	Simpson, W. H.	1015	Woods, J. H.
902	Wall, H. G.	957	Acton, G. E.	1016	Cook, B.

No.	Name	No.	Name	No.	Name
1017	Nichols, J. W. J.	1074	Selby, F. W.	1131	King, D. C.
1018	Kimber, R. W.	1075	Howlett, H.	1132	Simpson, A. H.
1019	Fromings, G.	1076	Edwards, F. H.	1133	Craker, S. J. C.
1020	Rice, R. A.	1077	Jackson, P.		
1021	Speed, J. D. R.	1078	Boakes, H. H.	**January, 1941.**	
1022	Burdis, J. G.	1079	Hurdman, A. S.	1134	Sim, R. H.
		1080	Hall, W.	1135	Brown, H.
November, 1940.		1081	Pohtson, R. H.	1136	Nil
1023	Hardy, L. G.	1082	Williams, T. A.	1137	Stoffel, W. J.
1024	Goodger, E.	1083	Rowe, P. W. V.	1138	Page, J. A.
1025	Quinell, G. A. V.	1084	Reynolds, L. E.	1139	Allen, B. G.
1026	Derbyshire, E. C.			1140	Whitley, B. R. E.
1027	White, W. T.	**December, 1940.**		1141	Cobley, A. P. M.
1028	Paddon, F. D.	1085	Rawling, J. H. C.	1142	Penfold, A. R.
1029	Preece, O. T.	1086	Mock, K.	1143	Price, R. A.
1030	Giles, F.	1087	Gilham, C. E.	1144	Russell, D.
1031	Hirst, H. E.	1088	Ballard, A. T.	1145	Summers, J. M.
1032	Fuggle, A. S.	1089	Bennett, R. W.	1146	Taylor, A.
1033	Ovens, A. L.	1090	Tice, A. E.	1147	Collins, C. C.
1034	Enock, A. E.	1091	Warrington, E.	1148	Berriman, B. H.
1035	Halliday, W. G.	1092	Glenville, R. W. H.	1149	Monks, C. A.
1036	Wilson, T.	1093	Russell, F. M.	1150	Clark, A. V.
1037	Bray, C. J. E.	1094	Speed, M. J. D.	1151	Colvin, K. J.
1038	Wisdom, C. A.	1095	Russell, S.	1152	McCalle, K. V.
1039	White, A. E. O.	1096	Greer, F. F.	1153	Burton, H. F.
1040	Eglinton, E.	1097	Smith, C.	1154	Steel, C. T.
1041	Crowley, E. W.	1098	Costin, E. G.	1155	Lawrence, W. A.
1042	Sitters, R. V.	1099	Winslade, G. S.	1156	Humphries, A. E.
1043	Bennett, J. W.	1100	Foreman, C. W.	1157	Jordan, K. J.
1044	Lindley, E. H.	1101	Paffett, W.	1158	Richards, A. G.
1045	Preston, A. U.	1102	Banyard, P. H.	1159	Brady, J. G.
1046	Bassam, R. A. U.	1103	Thomas, E. H.	1160	Brady, J. T.
1047	Cole, P. O.	1104	Norgate, A. E.	1161	Rottenburg, L. C.
1048	Palmer, D. H.	1105	Olds, A. W.	1162	Weekly, J. W.
1049	O'Connell, P.	1106	Price, A. R.	1163	Day, C.
1050	Thomson, P. R.	1107	Sheppard, A. W.	1164	Wright, W. F.
1051	Smart, H. W.	1108	Smith, F.	1165	Sherwood, R. F.
1052	Osborn, W. A.	1109	Morgan, C.	1166	Soper, J. P.
1053	Taylor, S. W. H.	1110	Harding, T. H.	1167	Wills, S. F.
1054	Stone, R.	1111	Nichols, E. R.	1168	Vidler, D. O.
1055	Nicolle, E. C.	1112	Brady, W. J.	1169	Mattholii, L. K.
1056	Jones, G. S.	1113	Weatherall, S. A.	1170	Whitehead,
1057	Banks, A.	1114	Hayke, F. L.		E. A. J.
1058	Whitson, D. J. W.	1115	Maskens, D. F.	1171	Hodgson, L. E.
1059	Biggenden, G. W.	1116	Walpole, W. G.	1172	Nineham, F. E.
1060	Cox, P. K.	1117	Ashford, A. V.	1173	Dacombe, W. F.
1061	Farey, G. A.	1118	Howard, M. E.	1174	Titchmarsh, F.
1062	Bark, F. L.	1119	Zealey, W. J.	1175	Sturman, H. D.
1063	McHardy, C.	1120	Hicks, I.	1176	Eve, W. M.
1064	Fleet, K.	1121	Barry, M.	1177	Sharpe, J. R.
1065	Fox, G. S.	1122	Seton, R. C.	1178	Scudamore, H. W.
1066	Kemp, C. G.	1123	Hurd, G. R.	1179	O'Brien, H. P.
1067	Matthews, L. S.	1124	Cowling, P. R.	1180	Ratcliffe, W. G.
1068	Snelgrove, P.	1125	Lidstone, J. R.	1181	Rosenthal, P. J.
1069	Coltman, K. A. S.	1126	Farnham, P. J.	1182	Coward, R. A.
1070	Redston, G.	1127	Walker, A.	1183	Ingle, E.
1071	Baldwin, R.	1128	Somers, F. W.	1184	Harrison, M. J.
1072	Baker, R. F.	1129	George, E. A.	1185	Best, R. H.
1073	Horobin, C. S.	1130	Hallford, H.	1186	Yaxley, F. A.

[55]

No.	Name	No.	Name	No.	Name
1187	Clark, A. S.	1243	Record, F.	1301	Hayter, D. E.
1188	Clark, R. P.	1244	Stone, B.	1302	Lovell, R. A.
1189	Cheeseman, A.	1245	Wilkie, A. S.	1303	Gidley, R. A.
1190	Basham, C. R.	1246	Legge, C. A.	1304	Filler, A. P.
1191	Treable, A. T.	1247	Knight, C. J.	1305	Christie, J. A.
1192	Gibbs, S. W.	1248	Jones, W. A.	1306	Winchcombe, J.R.
1193	Langley, R. J.	1249	Howe, F. G.	1307	Annett, A. E.
1194	Musson, H. E.	1250	Wakelin, J.	1308	West, F.
1195	Riches, R. H.	1251	Palin, F. J.	1309	Underwood, L. C
1196	Hall, J. R.	1252	Wood, P. J.	1310	Molyneux, P.
1197	Smith, J. E.	1253	Hawkes, R. C. R.	1311	Jenner, H. W.
1198	Elliott, A.	1254	Thomas, E. D.	1312	Rubie, E. H.
1199	Slough, F. C.	1255	Ironside, E. E.	1313	Whitehouse, L. J.
1200	Cheshire, D. A.	1256	Clement, L. G.	1314	Holt, E. G. S.
1201	Aked, R. F.	1257	Crowhurst, R. F.	1315	Pett, H.
1202	Barclay, F. E.	1258	Olde, E. A.	1316	Hills, A. F.
1203	Wallace, F. M.	1259	Brookes, R. H.	1317	Nimmo, R. S. E.
1204	Smith, D. A. G.	1260	Falle, J. L.	1318	Hendry, I. J.
1205	Smith, A.	1261	Ling, H. T.	1319	Woodward, F. H.
1206	Cox, E. C.	1262	Todd, C. W.	1320	Bartlett, A. C.
1207	Wilkie, J. D. S.	1263	Plater, G.	1321	Newman, W. T.
1208	Freeman, J. A.	1264	Record, H. G.	1322	Mann, L. E.
1209	Hatton, F. V.	1265	Felton, W. A.	1323	Egleton, R. F.
1210	Fox, D. H.	1266	Walton, G. E.	1324	Gentle, H. H.
1211	Ledger, P. G.	1267	Edwards, S. T.	1325	Gentle, E. G.
1212	Hitchcock, H. J.	1268	Beer, K. E.	1326	Gentle, H. W. J.
1213	May, E. C.	1269	North, F. E.	1327	Brown, J. A.
1214	Wilson, H. G.	1270	Humphreys,	1328	Aplin, F. S. W.
1215	Paffett, J.		J. R. F.	1329	Johnson, H. E.
1216	Adams, R. R. W.	1271	Shewbridge, A. T.	1330	Jones, D. O.
1217	Russell, G. A.	1272	Leonard, H. J.	1331	Dann, W. T.
1218	Swyer, C.	1273	Bilham, H. C.	1332	Hobbs, G. A.
1219	Watson, W.	1274	Wakelin, J. E.	1333	Fisher, J. J.
1220	Easterfield, J.	1275	Rixon, W. E.	1334	Cooke, K.
1221	Britton, A.	1276	Gorton, R. E.	1335	Wood, G. G.
1222	Joy, D. A.	1277	Wannop, L. E.	1336	Drew, H. G.
1223	Boorman, J. R.	1278	Foster, R. H.	1337	Noble, G. S.
1224	Warwick, D.	1279	Dixon, W. A.	1338	Withycombe,
1225	Caie, J. N.	1280	Dennis, C. C.		R. L.
1226	Voyce, E. D.	1281	Terry, R. G.	1339	Slythe, F.
1227	Dowding, W. G.	1282	Miles, C. P.	1340	Shingleton, J. T.
1228	Burgess, F. R.	1283	Waters, R. O.	1341	Chapman, J. J.
1229	Denman, C. M.	1284	Bayes, W.	1342	Hazelwood, A. C
1230	Collins, J. T.	1285	Waters, E.	1343	Haisman, H. D.
1231	Hamon, E. V.	1286	Corkery, T. R.	1344	Collis, G. A.
1232	Marchant, H. T.	1287	Messenger, A. G.	1345	Price, L. C.
1233	Coleman, M. H.	1288	Jeffs, P. G.	1346	Newman, R. R.
1234	Whitaker, R. A.	1289	Rogers, A. T.	1347	Deason, R. S.
		1290	Searles, H. S.	1348	Perkins, W. G.
February, 1941.		1291	Burford, P. C.	1349	Baker, L. C. J.
1235	Day, D.	1292	Harwood, H. J.	1350	Goodhew, A. R.
1236	Whitehart,	1293	Skinner, F. W. J.	1351	Smedley, D.
	R. C. G.	1294	Taylor, G. D.	1352	Howes, A. F.
1237	Dadley, H. E.	1295	Davis, G. W.	1353	Ball, S. J.
1238	Buckingham, C.	1296	Elmslie, W.	1354	Edmonds, J.
1239	Reeves, N. P.	1297	Brunner, L. W.	1355	Scott, R. A. L.
1240	Noonan, S.	1298	Ward, C. W.	1356	Payne, G. A.
1241	Harrison, A. A.	1299	Twomey, R. E.	1357	Pascoe, D. J.
1242	Bloss, R. G.	1300	Conway, J. S.	1358	Adley, A. J.

No.	Name	No.	Name	No.	Name
1359	Bogen, G. A.	1418	Pettitt, L. A.	1472	Thorpe, G. H.
1360	Davy, D. A.	1419	Harris, G. N.	1473	Vousden, H. C.
1361	Lovell, E. H. U.	1420	Weeks, J. R. T.	1474	Burningham,
1362	Bennett, T.	1421	Harkins, C. J.		H. W.
1363	Woolford, S. F.	1422	Whybrow, G. E.	1475	Willis, A. E.
1364	Bradford, E. A.	1423	Goodall, R. R. P.	1476	Cremore, H. G.
1365	Celia, C. W.	1424	Milton, D. G.	1477	Jones, W. C.
1366	Walker, R. G.	1425	Henning, J.	1478	Howe, W. R.
1367	Kavanagh, H.	1426	Pollard, L. W.	1479	Stinson, H. J. E.
1368	McIntosh, J. A.	1427	Towell, W. E.	1480	Lee, W. C.
1369	Barker, L. C	1428	Francis, W. W.	1481	Richards, N. O.
1370	Archer, H.	1429	Covett, A. T.	1482	Crowhurst,
1371	Graham, S. W. F.	1430	Lee, T. R.		E. H. G.
1372	Spooner, A. T.	1431	Potter, D. J.	1483	Efkin, G.
1373	Anderson, A. B.	1432	Day, A. C.	1484	Moffatt, T.
1374	Pocock, J. W.	1433	Button, R. H.	1485	Parker, R. A.
1375	Hawkins, H. J.	1434	Humphrey, S. F.	1486	Harper, T. C.
1376	Ayling, A. E.	1435	Ingram, J. H. T.	1487	Cole, W. H.
1377	Denby, P. B.	1436	Aldous, D. F.	1488	Hewer, C. J.
1378	Mann, G. H.	1437	Wedderburn, F. A.	1489	Wilson, J. T.
1379	Burbridge, G. W.	1438	Elliott, T. C.	1490	Aers, F. L.
1380	Burbridge, T. G.	1439	Gregory, T. H.	1491	Hawkins, G. A.
1381	Lucas, J. S.	1440	Newman, R. J.	1492	Mays, A. G.
1382	Collins, N. E.	1441	McCullagh, H.	1493	Humm, A. W.
1383	James, S. F.	1442	Geddes, E. A.	1494	Mungearn, W. A.
1384	Hilling, A. J. J.	1443	Linfield, R. S.	1495	Freye, D. W.
1385	Morley, B. T.	1444	Wilson, J.	1496	Pettigrew, W.
1386	Watson, H. C.	1445	Baker, A. S.	1497	Hastings, L. J.
1387	Brookes, R. A.	1446	King, C. J.	1498	Dixon, G. L.
1388	Lawrence, F.	1447	Harman, C.	1499	Coombes, B.
1389	Groom, C. G.	1448	Button, H. J.	1500	Wright, W. J.
1390	Osborne, R.	1449	Bond, G. A. A.	1501	Edgar, A. M.
1391	King, L. R.	1450	Shepherd, L. R. A.	1502	Patty, F. G.
1392	South, C. W.			1503	Sayer, E. W.
1393	Chard, P. J.	**March, 1941.**		1504	Swan, W. J.
1394	Campbell, I. M.	1451	Stevens, R. I.	1505	Nelson Marshall,
1395	Thornton, A.	1452	Tamlyn, B. H.		E. C.
1396	Cummins, W. E.	1453	Wright, W. J.	1506	Turner, C. E. F.
1397	Amos, E. J.	1454	Checksfield, H. W.	1507	Cherry, D. C.
1398	Waddington, W.B.	1455	Luck, E. A.	1508	Whibley, H. A.
1399	Stokes, J. D.	1456	Fromings, W. R.	1509	Carman, G. J.
1400	Bloomfield, A. E.	1457	Clark, R. S.	1510	McNaughton,
1401	Towell, W. T.	1458	Crossland, E.		A. R.
1402	Seward, W. G.	1459	Watkins, P. S.	1511	Smith, J.
1403	Knott, A.	1460	Edenborough,	1512	Gunner, H. S.
1404	Tipper, H. J.		J. B. D.	1513	Chatters, H. E.
1405	Robinson, H. J.	1461	McClory,	1514	Johnson, J.
1406	Goodwin, F.		D. T. P. O'D.	1515	Cox, A. G.
1407	Tolfrey, F. C.	1462	Wilson, A.	1516	Pavey, F. W.
1408	Rolfe, H. T.	1463	Fletcher, H. C.	1517	Rozier, E. E.
1409	Kay, W. C.	1464	Parry, G. W. F.	1518	Churchett, F. M.
1410	Ward, F. G.	1465	Corkery, D. F. F.	1519	Thomas, R. I.
1411	Harrison, G. F.	1466	Berryman, H. Q.	1520	Organ, C.
1412	Bugden, J.	1467	White, A. R.	1521	Fowler, A. E.
1413	Yardley, G. W.	1468	Hartley, W. K.	1522	Grinham, L. A.
1414	Silk, Jnr., T. J.	1469	Slark, W. H.	1523	Webb, J. J. O.
1415	Rayner, P. D.	1470	Newman, E. C.	1524	Hope, F.
1416	Williams, A.	1471	Birmingham,	1525	Reynolds, L. G.
1417	Bailey, R. T.		H. W.	1526	Raper, G. F

[57]

No.	Name	No.	Name	No.	Name
1527	Bishop, D. G.	1582	Hutchings, N. W.	1639	Smith, R. L.
1528	Godwin, W. D.	1583	Hemming, J. H. T	1640	Cleeves, D.
1529	Ablett, J. S.	1584	Plummer, W. H.	1641	Drayson, A. A.
1530	Pack, D. E.	1585	Higginson, H.	1642	Russell, L. J.
1531	Braby, G. H. P.	1586	Pointer, C. G.	1643	Hiscock, H.
1532	Storey, G. W.	1587	Goldberg, H.	1644	Dally, L.
1533	Norton, D. B.	1588	Westwood, W. L.	1645	Pickering, F. S.
1534	Miles, B. W.	1589	Britton, T. H. E.	1646	Guildford, E. T. G
1535	Littlechild, D.	1590	Voller, R.	1647	McMichael, H.
1536	Feast, H. J. P.	1591	Easter, C. M.	1648	Stenton, P. E.
1537	Higgs, D. E.	1592	Donovan, D. C.	1649	Wannenburg,
1538	Hudley, C. A.	1593	Kirage. D. J.		W. F.
1539	Hampton, F.	1594	Watkins, G. R.	1650	Graham, H. J.
1540	Higgins, J.	1595	Craker, H.	1651	Dawe, L. G.
1541	Casey, J.	1596	Stevens, P.	1652	Rendell, S. G.
1542	Dance, A. E.	1597	Calvert, N.	1653	Dove, J. M.
1543	Sales, J.	1598	Horsey, W.	1654	Jones, E. J.
1544	Smith, B. S.	1599	Chich, H. J.	1655	Skinner, W.
1545	Cripps, J.	1600	Pasterfield, R. H.	1656	Barlow, J.
1546	Ford, F. R.	1601	Wilkins, A. J.	1657	Plail, W. C.
1547	Humphries, A. E.	1602	Burnett, J. W.	1658	
1548	Tooke, H. S.	1603	Livermore, R.	to	} Nil
1549	Deacon, G. E.	1604	Rayner, S. J.	1667	
1550	Hiscock, D. D.	1605	Cole, G. E.	1668	Fitzpatrick, C. W
1551	Bratton, G.	1606	Tidbury, A.	1669	Payne, P. F.
1552	Marriott, W. B.	1607	Putnam, F. L.	1670	Wragg, G. E.
1553	Goddard, A. E.	1608	Criffield, H. E.	1671	Waters, H. S.
1554	Jeffreys, W. P.	1609	Sharp, R. T.	1672	Wright, E. A.
1555	Hopper, A. F.	1610	O'Donnell, P. J.	1673	Weller, J. S.
1556	Varney, K. W.	1611	Allchin, G. T.	1674	Selby, D. G.
1557	Haley, L. S.	1612	Flannery, F. E.	1675	King, A. J.
1558	Campbell, S. G.	1613	Hassall, C. J.	1676	Cook, R.
1559	Smithard, J. E.	1614	Feagan, T.	1677	Barnes, R. A.
1560	Shields, J. E. M.	1615	Glenn, W.	1678	Ramshow, S. W.
1561	Parrott, K. J.	1616	Simpson, C. F.	1679	Colburn, L. S.
1562	Wainwright, R. A	1617	Goodall, J. H.	1680	Hillcard, S.
1563	Robertson,	1618	Charles, A. F.	1681	Aikins, E. R. M.
	I. C. W.	1619	O'Dell, R. E.	1682	Harding, J. D.
1564	O'Byrne, J. J.	1620	Fordham, E. G.	1683	Benham, G. W.
1565	Clouder, A. E.	1621	Francis, D. B.	1684	Shurey, K. E. A.
1566	Knott, R. R. D. B.	1622	Dalley, O.	1685	Morter, W. F.
1567	Hope, G.	1623	Taylor, J.	1686	Ashdown, H.
1568	Young, A. T.	1624	Young, E. D.	1687	Tebbutt, J. R.
1569	Gladwin, W. T.	1625	Ford, A. A.	1688	Bratton, D.
1570	Skinner, H. S.	1626	Hamer, W. B.	1689	Dale, R. H.
1571	Sommers, L.	1627	Chick, E. R.	1690	Cross, F. F.
1572	Logan, K. H.	1628	Garnham, R. J. H.	1691	Belfield, F. S.
1573	Brett, G. M.	1629	Gooch, J. C.	1692	King, A. E.
		1630	Arbon, H. G.	1693	Church, A. E.
April, 1941.		1631	Pope, T. A. C.	1694	Nil
1574	Ralph, L. R.			1695	Plail, J. A.
1575	Anderson, D. J.	**May, 1941.**		1696	Ellis, F. J.
1576	Burbridge, E. A.	1632	Longlands, D.	1697	Robjant, A. J.
1577	Wood, G. E.	1633	Doubleday, E.	1698	Hill, J. D.
1578	Crossman,	1634	Kirk, H. L.	1699	Barrett, H. C.
	G. E. P.	1635	Chapman, D. W. J	1700	Jarvis, A. G.
1579	Nicholls, G. H.	1636	Brown, L.	1701	Pegrain, S.
1580	Whitney, G. F.	1637	Holland, R.	1702	Wright, S. V.
1581	Lamperd, D. A.	1638	Glover, W.	1703	Maynard, K. F.

No.	Name	No.	Name	No.	Name
1704	Wright, P. G.	1758	Smith, S.	1815	Hill, J.
1705	Jones, R. D.	1759	Stringer, M. S.	1816	Belam, E. C.
1706	O'Grady, R. E.	1760	Pearson, A. H.	1817	Kennedy, S. P.
1707	Goldsmith, H. D.	1761	Cook, A.	1818	Wells, H. G.
1708	Harris, P. J.	1762	Morley, A.	1819	Goodman, L. G.
1709	Harper, E. J.	1763	Cooper, C.	1820	Brady, F. S.
1710	Igglesden, A. R.	1764	King, G. W.	1821	Billinge, A. C.
1711·	Morbin, A. W.	1765	Sturgeon, R. G. W	1822	Humphried, M.
1712	Holton, P.	1766	Sullivan, D. D.	1823	Wilson, R. A. C.
1713	Harley, C. C.	1767	Lockley, F. B.	1824	Powell, A. A.
1714	Neate, F. H.	1768	Mead, A. E.	1825	Burten, L.
1715	Bustard, G. F.	1769	Addison, H. J.	1826	Burten, C.
1716	Shepherd, S. F.	1770	Gaum, C. B.	1827	Cartwright, L. F.
		1771	Challiss, W. H.	1828	Scarlett, W. A.
June, 1941.		1772	Howes, J. S.	1829	Garlick, E. R.
1717	Chadwick, R. G.	1773	Everest, D. J.	1830	Thomas, J. R.
1718	Green, J. H.	1774	Edmunds, S.	1831	Clarke, A. B.
1719	Blakeley, D.	1775	Marchant, L.H.G.	1832	Smith, W. J. R.
1720	Baker, R. E.	1776	Newman, W.	1833	Clark, M. S.
1721	Cordrey, E.	1777	Cruttenden, F.	1834	Sturgeon, R. H.
1722	Edmeades, W. M.	1778	Bourne, C. A. F.	1835	Patterden, J. B. F.
1723	Chave, F. V.	1779	Clark, W. G.	1836	Moore, H.
1724	Jatter, F. E.	1780	Welfare, H.	1837	Cane, H.
1725	Jennings, G. H.	1781	Carter, K. A.	1838	Gregory, C. J. W.
1726	Wickham, T. J.	1782	Trigg, G. H.	1839	Frost, R. W.
1727	Stannard, J.	1783	Kenward, H.	1840	Sherwin, K. L.
1728	Scarlett, S. W.	1784	Gregory, G. J.		
1729	Martin, E.	1785	Jennings, V. A.	**September, 1941.**	
1730	Bayden, W. J.	1786	Soper, T. P.	1841	Howell, D. J.
1731	Brooker, W. E. G.	1787	Brant, H. V.	1842	Staunton, B.
1732	Windett, H. F.	1788	Le Seflleur, D.	1843	Gregory, T.
1733	Taylor, H. G.	1789	Leeks, C. R. G.	1844	Cole, K. H.
1734	Turnell, A. D. P.	1790	Ewen, J. H.	1845	Powell, R.
1735	Higgins, R.	1791	Elliott, W.	1846	Maynard, A. W.
1736	Adams, J. F.	1792	Branley, G. O.	1847	Cowell, C. P.
1737	Webb, A. H.	1793	Kingston, C. H.	1848	Powell, P. J.
1738	Tuck, J. E.	1794	Clarke, A. W. M.	1849	Lawrence, G.
1739	Allan, D. W.	1795	Foy, A. E. C.	1850	Pilbrow, P. C. J.
1740	Hetherington,			1851	Gregory, D. W.
	F. N.	**August, 1941.**		1852	Cox, L. K.
1741	Sterry, A.	1796	Stimson, W. E. J.	1853	Aldington, S. W.
1742	Clare, E.	1797	Monks, R. W. M.	1854	Nicholls, W.
1743	Dewey, N. S.	1798	Rawson, A. F.	1855	Moore, A. H.
1744	Troubridge, H. G.	1799	Pope, J. H.	1856	Holliday, P. J.
1745	Camlin, H. W.	1800	Wilson, C. S.	1857	Wickenden, G. W
1746	Glover, C. A.	1801	Mountjoy,G.C.W.	1858	Simpson, W. M.
1747	Samuels, J. W. H.	1802	Valentine, L. E.	1859	Peerless, H· H. M.
		1803	Mason, C.	1860	Finnimore, G.
July, 1941.		1804	Sayers, R. A. V.	1861	Nutkins, P. A·
1748	Holder, D.	1805	Short, C. F.	1862	Neal, D. J.
1749	Relf, R. L.	1806	Tucker, E.	1863	Riley, M.
1750	Sherwill, H. C.	1807	Plumm,·G. K.	1864	Farr, F. T.
1751	Leather, J. S.	1808	Codling, F. E.	1865	Simpson, A. E.
1752	Laidler, R. M.	1809	Harvey, M. W.	1866	Sudlow, W.
1753	Putnam, H. G.	1810	Gregory, H. G.	1867	Rodgers, A. E.
1754	Travis, E. G.	1811	Green, A. E.	1868·	Roberts, C. J.
1755	Bowden, E. F.	1812	Robinson, C. H.	1869	Gledhill, J. W.
1756	Hards, C. O.	1813	Freeman, H.	1870	Bucknell, V. P.
1757	Bax, D. R. C.	1814	Tasker, J. A.	1871	Lee, K. O.

No.	Name	No.	Name	No.	Name
1872	Harman, W.	1928	Smith, K. J.	1983	Searchfield, G. P.
1873	Holden, E. J.	1929	Sherriff, D. A.	1984	Lilley, L. D.
1874	Kitton, D. F.	1930	Broucke, H. P.	1985	Moore, C. W.
1875	Spiby, R. G.	1931	Tickner, A. J. W.	1986	Debonnaire, P. H.
1876	Rayner, A. H.	1932	Collyer, K. S.	1987	Moore, A. C
1877	Mogan, J.	1933	Doughty, J. H.	1988	Ascoli, A.
1878	Evans, O.	1934	Addison, G.	1989	Flack, H. M.
1879	Hadfield, E. G.	1955	Trueman, W.	1990	Hughes, F.
1880	Dabin, A. W.	1956	James, F. W.	1991	Gore, F. S.
1881	Bennett, F.			1992	Wood, K. W.
1882	Goodger, R. O.	**November, 1941.**		1993	Meiklereid, K.
1883	Fullerton, S. G.	1937	Stuart, E. W.	1994	Reed, H. J.
1884	Kennett, H. P.	1938	Vincent, A. G.	1995	Raiman, A. T.
1885	Way, A. W.	1939	Tatum, A. E.	1996	Tibble, A.
1886	Dixon, E. N. E.	1940	Goodchild, J. C.	1997	Mullerby, J. E.
1887	Smith, H. W.	1941	Tuff, J. H.	1998	Light, D. G.
1888	Bratton, E.	1942	Everest, R.	1999	Alexander, C. E.
1889	Marrable, R. R.	1943	Bumstead, F. P.	2000	Nil
1890	Joyce, E. J. C.	1944	Bath, A. W.	2001	Nil
1891	Connor, A. D. J.	1945	Bathes, A. M.	2002	Nil
1892	Smith, H. J.	1946	Roberts, J. A.	2003	Holden, C. W.
1893	Cardinal, A. W.	1947	Silverthorne, L. J.	2004	Turner, C. A.
1894	Morris, W. J.	1948	Castellan, S. P.	2005	Jumpsen, C. W.
1895	Andrews, D. N.	1949	Vaile, S.	2006	Maddison, F. P.
1896	Porter-Smith, P. R.	1950	Brown, H.	2007	Hills, A. F.
		1951	Woolston, T.	2008	Collins, E. A.
1897	Osborne, J.	1952	Austin, H.	2009	Reynolds, R.
1898	Carpenter, E. C.	1953	Aveling, F.	2010	Clements, J.
1899	Wright, C. H.	1954	Coombes, H. E.	2011	Carver, D. W.
1900	Walker, J. C.	1955	Debonnaire, J. S.	2012	White, A.
1901	Carter, F. C.	1956	Vass, L. E.	2013	Steptoe, F. W.
1902	Gibson, J. H.	1957	Ecott, C. R.	2014	Powell, D. E.
1903	Jarvis, E. J.	1958	Storch, C.	2015	Dalton, A. H.
1904	Coltham, E. A.	1959	Moore, P. W.	2016	Mays, R.
1905	Hibbett, E. C.	1960	Cooper, R. W. J.	2017	Jones, N. F.
		1961	Gale, S. E.	2018	Smith, G. H.
October, 1941.		1962	Hulk, F. W.	2019	Dean, P. L.
1906	Bates, D.	1963	Riley, G. T.	2020	Rose, G. H.
1907	Geddie, H. J. D.	1964	Preece, J. J.	2021	Starr, T.
1908	Stevens, E.	1965	Comport, A. L.	2022	Webb, L.
1909	Harvey, G. S. A.	1966	Attwood, A. J.	2023	Moss, J.
1910	Powell, D. B.	1967	Franck, M. L.	2024	Murphy, J.
1911	Clitherow, A. C. J.	1968	Caxton, C. H.	2025	Morgan, W.
1912	Olivo, A. A.	1969	Blake, C. D.	2026	Butcher, W.
1913	Quinton, J. E.	1970	Grizzell, R. E.	2027	Leggett, G. H.
1914	Gleeson, M. C.	1971	Hopkins, L.	2028	Alston, J.
1915	McLachlan, K. A.	1972	Hardy, C. A.	2029	Cock, J. J.
1916	Punchard, A. P.	1973	Eliff, A. H.	2030	De Gier, P. R.
1917	Biggs, A. T.	1974	Spears, G. H.	2031	Lawrence, D. L.
1918	Edmead, E.	1975	Nil	2032	Golding, F. W.
1919	Davis, P. A.	1976	Hillier, F. N.		
1920	Brocks, B. J.	1977	Hancock, D. D.	**January, 1942.**	
1921	Easthope, W. F.	1978	Bowes, H. A.	2033	Boyd, G. M.
1922	Bright, F. E.	1979	Chandler, S.	2034	Mabbs, C. P.
1923	White, W. G.	1980	Spiers, H. C.	2035	Varney, A. M.
1924	Poston, A. B.			2036	Hunt W.
1925	Burgess, A. H.	**December, 1941.**		2037	Hopton, J.
1926	Ibbotson, F.	1981	Mytton, J. A.	2038	Yolland, R. H.
1927	Woodward, E.	1982	Goulding, R.	2039	Drew, A. M.

No.	Name	No.	Name	No.	Name
2040	Sharp, E.	2097	New, W. J.	2154	Winwood, R. A.
2041	Golding, A. E.	2098	Kew, L. E. H.	2155	Pedley, H. G. W
2042	Abel, A. B.	2099	Cooper, G. S.	2156	McLeod, C. T.
2043	Enz, E. C.	2100	Ruffle, G. G.	2157	Foster, E.
2044	Lloyd, R.	2101	Ellis, M. F.	2158	Blows, H. A.
2045	Simpson, L. F.	2102	Tether, H. J.	2159	Clarke, F. E.
2046	Lock, H. W.	2103	Lowe, N. H.	2160	Baldry, H. S. G.
2047	Benstead, G. A.	2104	Avery, M. J.	2161	Rayner, C.
2048	Jenkinson, A. V.	2105	Boxall, S. G.	2162	Marchant, R. W.
2049	Wyatt, A. J.	2106	Harris, A. P.	2163	Catlett, V. C.
2050	Walker, H. H.	2107	Schipper, G. E.	2164	Willson, W. H.
2051	Davis, C. E.	2108	Smith, H. E.	2165	Latham, C. R.
2052	Knight, R. C.	2109	Ednie, R. W.	2166	Davey, G. J.
2053	Wade, A. A.	2110	Robertson, J. W.	2167	Malkin, R. A.
2054	Goulding, W. H.	2111	Nair, H. E.	2168	Turner, A. G.
2055	Tharme, J. E.	2112	Walker, E. A.	2169	Codling, F.
2056	Grandfield, S. J.	2113	Crowest, J. P.	2170	Cater, D. R.
2057	Frooms, A. V.	2114	Boakes, G.	2171	Jones, H. G.
2058	Daniel, W.	2115	Fearon, S. A.	2172	Shurety, R. P.
2059	Gibbs, A. E.	2116	Wyatt, J. A. F.	2173	Scriven, K.
2060	Payne, L. J.	2117	Walker, A. A. A.	2174	Flack, E. E.
2061	Murray, W. A.	2118	Meyer, W. F.	2175	Wheeler, S.
2062	Lawson, R. E.	2119	Harrild, A. E.	2176	Meade, C. J.
2063	Smith, E.	2120	Merrett, E. C.	2177	Wilson, E. W.
2064	Pearce, G.	2121	Daniels, A.	2178	Grover, E.
2065	Russell, G.	2122	Suttie, W. J.	2179	Locke, E.
2066	Davids, P. H.	2123	Nash, C. E. S.	2180	Foster, S. J.
2067	Patient, T. G.	2124	Holden, A. W. G.	2181	Bevan, J. H.
2068	Grout, W. D.	2125	Jenkins, E. G.	2182	Ford, E. C.
2069	Keen, C. D.	2126	Hamling, H. R.	2183	Fanthorpe, R.
2070	Moss, J. J.	2127	Hills, S. C.	2184	Glinister, A. C.
2071	Elliott, C. R.	2128	Woodward, J. S.	2185	Harley, D. S.
2072	Jeffries, C.			2186	Hilder, E. C.
2073	Nye, A. A.	**March, 1942.**		2187	Clark, A. S.
2074	Rogers, J.	2129	Pearson, J. F.	2188	Fordham, F. A.
		2130	Jeffery, R. W.	2189	Vaughan, L. W.
February, 1942.		2131	Hickey, J. W.	2190	Gomm, J. H.
2075	Harker, G. W.	2132	Lintill, W. H.	2191	Fitzpatrick, R. C.
2076	Allin, D. T.	2133	Williams, R. A.	2192	Jones, G. M.
2077	Francis, D. B.	2134	Dunn, G.	2193	Higginbottom, D. E.
2078	Whibley, J. R.	2135	Sayers, G. C.		
2079	Bagshaw, W. S.	2136	Braniff, G.	2194	Hewett, J. J.
2080	Horseman, C.	2137	Paffett, L. J.	2195	Dysart, C.
2081	Lidgley, C.	2138	Wilson, F. H.	2196	McLordson, F. H. L.
2082	Harrod, C. E. J.	2139	Dray, F. J. S.		
2083	Northfield, C. F.	2140	Inwood, D. R.	2197	Bowen, J. A.
2084	Harsant, H. S.	2141	Cornwell, F. R.	2198	Russell, J. C.
2085	Ballantyne, D. F.	2142	Ellis, P.	2199	Horton, R. R.
2086	Price, R. J.	2143	Norris, R. K.	2200	Savage, R. A. E.
2087	Lavell, F. C.	2144	Archer, R.	2201	Doak, E. N.
2088	Bumstead, G.	2145	Whettell, W. R. A.	2202	Ash, F. G.
2089	Hancock, F. C.	2146	Minifie, F. G.	2203	Addison, F. W.
2090	Povey, A.	2147	Carrington, H.	2204	Gregory, C. P.
2091	Marshall, W. T.	2148	Burton, J.	2205	Keeley, H. E.
2092	Bishop, G. T. E.	2149	Gardiner, P. W.	2206	Keyte, P. S.
2093	Acors, R. J.	2150	Crittenden, S. G.	2207	Cope, J. G.
2094	Barley, F. C.	2151	Reading, L. F.	2208	Low, A.
2095	Smith, W. C. H.	2152	Hornblow, R. J.	2209	Hoiles, T. W.
2096	Roberts, J. W.	2153	Jameson, R. L.	2210	Maynard, L. A.

No.	Name	No.	Name	No.	Name
2211	Rowe, B. S.	2268	Britton, F. L.	**May, 1942.**	
		2269	Ayres, L. L.	2327	Drew, W. B.
April, 1942.		2270	Jacob, D. B.	2328	Bowden, D. M.
2212	Collins, D. C.	2271	Smith, R. V.	2329	Darby, E. L.
2213	Green, J.	2272	Allen, C. G. C.	2330	Stevens, W. S.
2214	May, H. A. L.	2273	Stiff, R. A.	2331	Slatford, A. E.
2215	Wild, G.	2274	Norton, P. G. M.	2332	Martin, J. J. C.
2216	Robins, W. T.	2275	Smart, L. O.	2333	Throndsen, T. B.
2217	Hough, H. G.	2276	McNeil, N. T.	2334	Orbell, A. J.—
2218	Reynolds, P. J.	2277	Karn, S. J.	2335	Wilson, D. C.
2219	Butterworth, J. T.	2278	Green, C. G.	2336	Johnson, C. J.
2220	Prebble, E. R.	2279	Cooper, L. G.	2337	Bowe, F.
2221	Goldsworthy, A.	2280	Pickering, A. G.	2338	Stone, R. H.
2222	Breeze, C. E. E.	2281	Pyrke, H.	2339	Kyle, J. B.
2223	Brain, A. E.	2282	Tomkins, J. A. G.	2340	Nalyon, J. A.
2224	Wood, F. C. J.	2283	Winterton, L. C.		
2225	Long, H. A.	2284	Bogg, S. C.	**June, 1942.**	
2226	Ling, S. E.	2285	Dowler, D.	2341	Crompton, H. G.
2227	Scantlebury, R. C.	2286	Stansfield, F. G.	2342	Muir, C. W.
2228	Garlick, H.	2287	Redford, R. A.	2343	Jones, P. R.
2229	Browar, F. E.	2288	Hansford, B. H.	2344	Whitemall, J.
2230	Yendle, W. C.	2289	Lingwood, E.	2345	Martin, K. T.
2231	Green, C. G.	2290	Ashby, M.	2346	Talbot, E. S.
2232	Hickmore, J. G.	2291	Hancock, A. T.	2347	Pilbrow, J. E.
2233	Fisher, E. G.	2292	Douglas, A.	2348	Nicholls, E. A.
2234	Mortimore, H.	2293	Newcombe, H. S.	2349	Crampton, H. W
2235	Cutler, F. E.	2294	Basham, E.	2350	Roberts, E. L.
2236	Vickers, N.	2295	Humphrey, R. A.	2351	Henniker, M. H.
2237	Coster, W. F.	2296	Manvill, A. R.	2352	Banyan, W. C.
2238	French, E.	2297	Pollock, W.	2353	Hawes, H.
2239	Liles, W. S.	2298	Young, G. C	2354	Mason, V.
2240	Kentell, R. C.	2299	Jones, J.	2355	Startup, W. D.
2241	Tait, R. R.	2300	Lambert, H.		
2242	Nottage, L. W.	2301	Bodiam, G. H.	**July, 1942.**	
2243	Wall, E. S.	2302	Lerpiniere, H.	2356	Kerr, J. R.
2244	Cousins, W. E. E.	2303	Lang, H. G.	2357	Svenson, D.
2245	Bateman, F. A.	2304	Waite, J. J.	2358	Capel, J. W.
2246	Symons, R. W.	2305	Sharpe, K. W.	2359	Watts, W. H.
2247	King, R. G.	2306	Johnston, J. A.	2360	Hewitt, H. C.
2248	Craker, W. F.	2307	White, F. A.	2361	Hewitt, D. C.
2249	Alexander, F. S.	2308	Bennett, R. C.	2362	Haynes, D. R.
2250	Chandler, S. T.	2309	Humphreys, M.	2363	Dodsworth, A. T.
2251	Jenkin, V. G.	2310	White, M. H.	2364	Firminger, J. A.
2252	McMurray, A. W.	2311	Rose, A.	2365	Baldwin, S. J.
2253	Leach, W. J.	2312	Kemp, S. F.	2366	Hewitt, M.
2254	Hemming, G.W.T.	2313	Harris, E.	2367	Price, R. C.
2255	Humphries, H. H.	2314	Hall, E. G.	2368	Adnams, C. W.
2256	Mead, H. A.	2315	Bennett, W. A.	2369	Tilzey, G. S.
2257	Filmer, W. E.	2316	Spears, J. R.	2370	Hopkins, E. L.
2258	Harman, A. J.	2317	Wray, W.	2371	Bideleux, G. F.
2259	Yelland, R. C.	2318	Stenning, G. A.	2372	Carse, E. S.
2260	King, E. J.	2319	Hookway, H. G.	2373	Marritt, S. J.
2261	Ross, E. J.	2320	Williams, R. G.	2374	Westall, S. W.
2262	Eastcott, D. W.	2321	Hoberts, C.	2375	Dann, H. J.
2263	Dale, B. B.	2322	Bond, W. G.	2376	Gratwick, G. J.
2264	Pike, D. W.	2323	Pegrim, E.	2377	Ballin, C. C.
2265	Gilbert, R. F.	2324	Barlay, J. H.	2378	Lawrence, F. W.
2266	Gray, L. W.	2325	Davey, W. C.	2379	Frisby, T. J.
2267	Watts, L. R.	2326	Mitchell, E. W.		

No.	Name	No.	Name	No.	Name
2380	Hulbert, R. B.	2434	Hodder Williams, W. G.	2489	Ellis, R. A.
2381	Heaton, L. H.			2490	Dudley, A. G.
2382	Carter, A. H. P.	2435	Winter, J. A. V.	2491	Friend, J.
2383	Edwards, G. M.	2436	Filtness, R. J.	2492	Edmeades, R. L.
2384	Waters, C. J. E.	2437	Cope, M. V.	2493	Costin, G. W.
2385	O'Connell, L. P.	2438	Carse, J. O.	2494	Elliott, J. T.
2386	Jenn, L. R.	2439	Stapleton, A. R.	2495	Kennedy, J. A.
2387	Gibbs, D. W.	2440	Darling, J. J. A.	2496	Isles, H.
2388	Galloway, H. A.	2441	Donneley, E.	2497	Parsons, W. G.
2389	Hookway, R. G.	2442	Nunn, F.	2498	Neal, B. V.
2390	Knight, R. W.	2443	Vellenoweth, W. G.	2499	Whiting, A. E.
2391	Nevett, F. J.			2500	Moore, J. A.
2392	Twinberrow, J. D.	2444	Banks, D. J.	2501	Mayers, D. E.
2393	Worthington, B.	2445	Kanaar, H.	2502	Lewis, B. W.
		2446	Johnson, G. P.	2503	Warrington, R. J.
August, 1942.		2447	Smith, R. S.	2504	Verity, J. C.
2394	Boxwell, L. A.	2448	Randall, J. W. J.	2505	Sherwood, R. G.
2395	Arnold, E. R.	2449	Piper, H. C.	2506	Scott, W. G.
2396	Sparks, G. E. C.	2450	Barton, P. M.	2507	Davison, H. A.
2397	Gardener, L. R.	2451	Howes, R. H.	2508	Ambler, P. G.
2398	Sageman, W. E.	2452	Mackay, D. R. B.	2509	Burnhams, A. J.
2399	Pain, H. G. J.	2453	Box, D. R. C.	2510	Newton, K.
2400	Van Den Bergh, E.	2454	Short, J. D.	2511	Puckridge, C. E.
2401	Baker, A. P.	2455	Ferris, R.	2512	Easthope, D. H.
2402	Fletcher, R. R.	2456	Wallace, F. M.	2513	Humphreys, L. C.
2403	Ford, R. W.			2514	Joyce, T. D.
2404	Dabin, G. H.	**October, 1942.**		2515	Avis, G. H.
2405	Miller, F.	2457	Kitchener, J. A.	2516	Rainbow, K. W.
2406	Wilshaw, J. H. F.	2458	Ball, F. J.	2517	Brine, A. S. A.
2407	Harman, J.	2459	Matholie, P.	2518	Mayhew, R. C.
2408	Bowden, M. P.	2460	Beal, R. E.	2519	Sergeant, H. J.
2409	Philpott, S. E.	2461	Cox, N. J.	2520	Dempsey, P. J.
2410	Cooke, T. J.	2462	Jewhurst, W. J.	2521	Menet, F.
2411	Seaton, D. N.	2463	Goodman, G. F.	2522	Hobbs, R. G.
2412	Tayler, F. A. H.	2464	Seaman, W. B.	2523	Bowen, G. R.
2413	Arrowsmith, W. C	2465	Teasdale, J. L.	2524	McCleave, N.
2414	Wise, C. G.	2466	Stockley, L. F.	2525	Hooper, G. D.
2415	Finnis, R. A.	2467	Hull, A. R.	2526	Hastings, W. L.
2416	Worthington, S. F. D.	2468	Brimmer, R. E.	2527	Smith, W. J.
		2469	Sayers, R. A. V.	2528	Gullay, S. F.
2417	Edwards, S. J.	2470	Crook, G.	2529	Martin, A. S.
2418	Kemp, E. C.	2471	Grimshaw, J. H.	2530	Westlake, H. G.
2419	Fry, I. K.	2472	Gray, D. J.	2531	Burdis, R. H.
2420	Godsmark, C. T.	2473	Carr, C. F. G.	2532	Larkin, H. G.
2421	Daly, J.	2474	Harvey, T. H.	2533	Symes, L. F.
2422	Cook, R. A.	2475	Ham, C. J.	2534	Kimble, R. G.
2423	Gale, J. H.	2476	Chantrell, G. H.	2535	Emery, A.
2424	Rolfe, R. R. G.	2477	Hinds, C. W.	2536	Sullivan, T.
2425	Morton, W. H.	2478	Babbage, C. W.	2537	Hodges, C. A.
		2479	Novell, W. J.	2538	Clark, J. H. F.
September, 1942.		2480	Bodman, E.	2539	Hartwell, T.
2426	Griffiths, L. J.	2481	Burdick, B. S.	2540	Malin, W.
2427	Dennis, B.	2482	Freeman, A. E.	2541	Licence, F. W.
2428	Carrick, D.	2483	Donovan, D.	2542	Dighton, C.
2429	Catlin, W.	2484	Head, T. R.	2543	Steele, L. R.
2430	Everitt, G. W.	2485	Catling, T. H. H.	2544	Pavey, F. W.
2431	Shearring, G. L.	2486	Gregory, F. C.	2545	Horton, H. A.
2432	Pinnock, C. J. P.	2487	Rogers, T. W.	2546	Humphrey, W. A.
2433	Hitchcock, J. T.	2488	Jackson, A. F. A.	2547	Briault, L. D.

[63]

No.	Name	No.	Name	No.	Name
2548	Watts, E. L.	2604	Ives, R. G.	2660	Overton, W. H. T.
2549	Algar, R. H.	2605	Scheels, H. G. E.	2661	Green, W.
2550	Taylor, L.	2606	Fuller, R.	2662	Haines, C. T.
2551	Norton, L.	2607	Pearce, T. G.	2663	Cramp, A. A.
2552	Coombs, F. H.	2608	Knott, W. H.	2664	Pinkstone, J.
2553	Underwood, T. E.	2609	Meadowcroft,	2665	Parsons, G.
2554	Price, J. A.		D. R.	2666	Brigden, L. J.
2555	Finch, F. G.	2610	Etheridge, A. E.	2667	Alicoon, M.
2556	Waight, F.	2611	Naden, A. H.	2668	Maunder, P. W.
2557	Day, W. C.	2612	Skeggs, A. J.	2669	Gorton, S. R.
2558	Whiterod, R.	2613	Ansell, R. F.	2670	Cox, L. W. J.
2559	Russell, N. E.	2614	Tanner, C. S.	2671	Garner, F.
2560	Kent, S. C.	2615	Bauch, E.	2672	Corlay, W. H.
2561	Tilby, E. S.	2616	Burton, F. D.	2673	Wood, L. T.
2562	Halfpenny, J. T.	2617	Duke, S. W.	2674	Kemp, D. S.
2563	Kingston, F. W. S.	2618	Potterton, W. E.	2675	Baker, E. E.
2564	Peel, A.	2619	Hoile, W.	2676	Addison, S.
2565	Constant, L. D. E.	2620	Sheen, A. W.	2677	Badis, S.
2566	Huggett, A. O.	2621	Bulman, A. J.	2678	Gray, H. S.
2567	Wale, R. G.	2622	Morris, A. G.	2679	Welch, A.
		2623	Ouvry, N. D.	2680	Aiggar, A. D.
November, 1942.		2624	Mitchell, H. M.	2681	Amos, W.
2568	Weller, W.	2625	Pinder, L. F.	2682	Watts, H.
2569	Hoysted, C. W.	2626	Grover, R.	2683	Adams, H. F.
2570	Bardouleau,	2627	Combley, H.	2684	May, W. H.
	C. E. A.	2628	Marshall, S. G.	2685	Benoy, F. G.
2571	Stennett, W. J.	2629	Waite, W. H.	2686	Meehan, P.
2572	Dykes, G.	2630	Buckland, F. W.	2687	Kensington, J. M.
2573	Lewis, B.	2631	Packman, E. H.	2688	Brown, A. J.
2574	Nowrie, J.	2632	Whale, T. H.	2689	Whichelow, A. J.
2575	Jeal, A. J.	2633	Dadd, R. A.	2690	Cooper, L. H.
2576	Hoyles, A. W.	2634	Peacock, H. H.	2691	De Cordova, P.
2577	Duke, S. W.	2635	Knight, R.	2692	Pilton, F. W.
2578	Rhodes, D. H. J.			2693	Monkley, H. V.
2579	Castellano, F.	**December, 1942.**		2694	Cant, J. W. C.
2580	Freeman, J. A.	2636	Burrows, C. A.	2695	Churcher, W. T.
2581	Holton, H.	2637	Comber, R. E.	2696	Martin, F. R.
2582	Sharland, B. J.	2638	Grender, E. H.	2697	Parsons, A. F.
2583	Walter, H. J.	2639	Coe, D.	2698	Lettis, R. J.
2584	Nicholls, F. K.	2640	Wardle, F.	2699	Cooper, W. A.
2585	Kearns, J. F.	2641	Ricketts, M. R.	2700	Rawlings, F. A.
2586	Hartley, H. R.	2642	Taplin, W. R.	2701	Ellis, L. K.
2587	Mountjoy, J. H.	2643	Duncan, W. G.	2702	Baldwin, K. W.
2588	Lawrence, G. A.	2644	Harrod, P.	2703	Brown, F. L.
2589	Cox, S. C.	2645	Frid, W. C.	2704	Dixon, W. A.
2590	Smedley, J. S.	2646	Robinson, H. J.	2705	Bridgeland, J.
2591	Sisley, L.	2647	Child, G.		
2592	Tilby, J.	2648	Fraser, J. L.	**January, 1943.**	
2593	Griscoll, E. W.	2649	Baines, R.	2706	Gardner, S. J.
2594	Ogilvie, C. E.	2650	Balaam, H. B.	2707	Barry, J. C.
2595	Abrehart, W. F.	2651	Burt, A. E.	2708	Gray, F. H.
2596	Barnes, F. A.	2652	Andrews, R. H.	2709	Heath, J. E.
2597	French, E.	2653	Day, W. L. G.	2710	Anthony, C. F.
2598	Willis, D. T.	2654	Reilly, F. W.	2711	Barker, G. R.
2599	Apsley, L. J.	2655	Baker, G.	2712	Colyer, O. C.
2600	Hewson, W. A.	2656	Blackmore, R. A.	2713	Morgan, G. E. C.
2601	Kenward, P. G.	2657	Peters, A. E.	2714	Webley, W. L.
2602	Miller, H. T.	2658	Seal, A. S.	2715	Kenway, S. H.
2603	Brennan, A. S.	2659	Welch, S. E.	2716	Cooper, E. J.

No.	Name	No.	Name	No.	Name
2717	Baird, W. R.	2775	Cook, D.	2832	Folley, L. A.
2718	Anderson, B. R.	2776	Covington, T. A.	2833	Manton, W. F.
2719	Bostwick, A. B.	2777	Walsh, F. C.	2834	Baker, B. L.
2720	Bristow, R. G.	2778	Stock, S. R.	2835	Reekie, H. S.
2721	Bellis, A.	2779	Brown, W. C.	2836	Davies, L.
2722	Aveling, F. A.	2780	Bennett, K. G.	2837	Davey, H. L.
2723	Brand, K. J. M.	2781	Barker, S. L.	2838	Bunker, J.
2724	Collins, J. T.	2782	Corin, E. J. C.	2839	Bellsham, W. A
2725	Brown, E. C.	2783	Chance, L.	2840	Wells, H.
2726	Carey, S. C.	2784	Reed, L. D.	2841	Appleton, A. V.
2727	Bowditch, P. S.	2785	Duncan, E.	2842	Fisher, R. S. W.
2728	Armstrong, W.	2786	Boxall, C. W.	2843	Scudder, H.
2729	Brodrick, E. V.	2787	Bunce, A. G. M.	2844	Evans, G. A.
2730	Thurnell, D. P.	2788	Caton, S. A.	2845	Muir, A. F.
2731	Moody, A.	2789	Colvin, J. A.	2846	McBride, W. H.
2732	Mogan, J.	2790	Dunford, E. G.	2847	Campbell, D.
2733	Sievewright, R. S.	2791	Boyle, J. E.	2848	Cutchey, L. E.
2734	Hilton, E.	2792	Blowes, G. A.	2849	Cross, F. B.
2735	Parsons, S. J.	2793	Wood, A. C.	2850	Clarke, J. I. F.
2736	Oliver, A. B.	2794	Chapman, E. G.	2851	Dinan, H.
2737	Sims, L. C. J.	2795	Morris, H. W.	2852	Coombs, D. H.
2738	Davis, C. E.	2796	Furness, J. C. C.	2853	Golds, R. W.
2739	Cook, C. M.	2797	Krantz, D.	2854	Denning, J. H.
2740	Barrett, M. D.	2798	Gold, L.	2855	Dembrey, J. L.
2741	Drummond,	2799	Warman, L.	2856	Faulkner, A.
	M. L. A.	2800	Shelley, A. T.	2857	Batchelor, G. W.
2742	Cripps, C. L.	2801	Groom, J.	2858	Darrington, G. A.
2743	Baker, L. J.	2802	Allchorne, H. H.	2859	Bentley, A. E.
2744	Boakes, J. L.	2803	Wilkes, J. W.	2860	Dymond, W. S.
2745	Collyer, S. A.	2804	Werner, E. F.	2861	Jenner, A. J.
2746	Brockman, E. J.	2805	Davey, S. G.	2862	Wilkins, J. R.
2747	Adshead, H.	2806	Bailey, R. G.	2863	Cremer, R. J.
2748	Collier, G. R.	2807	Branch, S. A.	2864	Fitzalan, A. A.
2749	Howlett, S. G.	2808	Abrehart, F. T.	2865	Peat, H. T.
2750	Aust, W. S.	2809	Llewellyn, W. P.	2866	Densham, G. A.
2751	Wilson, A.	2810	Crisp, W. H.	2867	Argyle, H. C.
2752	Collins, F. W.	2811	Bennett, A. G. G.	2868	Harvey, G. C.
2753	Gordon, R. M.	2812	Dorsett, R. L.	2869	Greenwood, A.
2754	Bell, J. E.	2813	Dewar, T. G.	2870	Lock, A. L.
2755	Lunn, R. M.			2871	Chisholm, J. G.
2756	Fitter, N. J. C.	**February, 1943.**		2872	Carter, E. G.
2757	Gisboene, G. H. B.	2814	Fowle, E. H.	2873	Devall, G. A.
2758	Workman, J. D.	2815	Wilson, N. A.	2874	Honeyman, R. A
2759	Garrod, P. R.	2816	O'Sullivan, P.	2875	Nicholls, G. E.
2760	Summersby, S. T.	2817	Timbers, H. R.	2876	Greenaway, W.
2761	Jones, J. C.	2818	Duffin, A. J. G.	2877	Fife, A. C.
2762	Paris, F. J.	2819	Dudgeon, W. G.	2878	Doulton, W. G.
2763	Monteith, J. H.	2820	Dacey, B. D.	2879	Sear, J. W. T.
2764	Huckle, R.	2821	Keogh, D. W.	2880	Hasnip, G. W.
2765	Waters, C.	2822	Byron, J.	2881	Evans, F. A.
2766	Longhurst, A. J. J.	2823	Edmunds, B.	2882	Bryant, A. J.
2767	Shirley, A. T.	2824	Connop, W. S.	2883	Hodglin, F. A.
2768	Cox, F. H.	2825	Cable, C. F.	2884	Coles, S. B.
2769	Wright, B.	2826	Diaper, S.	2885	Balmforth, G. S.
2770	Bosher, S. A.	2827	Cozens, W. J.	2886	Gregory, W. H.
2771	Smith, E. S.	2828	Pollock, S. W. G.	2887	John, C. E.
2772	Smith, E. J.	2829	Fudge, F. A. C.		
2773	Dando, L. W.	2830	Frost, R. W. A.	**March, 1943.**	
2774	Denyer, E. E.	2831	Dixie, W. E. C.	2888	Parks, H. J.

No.	Name	No.	Name	No.	Name
2889	Hackett, S. V.	2948	Waller, W.	3004	Harnack, C. D.
2890	Gumbrill, C. F.	2949	White, J. T.	3005	Whitaker, F.
2891	Beater, R. C.	2950	Jefferies, W. T.	3006	Blakeley, R. C.
2892	Essex, G. H.	2951	Hammond, R. H.	3007	Holland, G. W.
2893	Harris, B.	2952	Longhurst, A. J.	3008	Kemp, D. G.
2894	Hardy, J. W.	2953	Dudley, A. E.	3009	Bush, J. H.
2895	Jameson, M. R.	2954	Hansher, H. C.	3010	Jennings, C. G.
2896	Grubb, W. J.	2955	Bunning, J. J.	3011	Lilley, B. F.
2897	Donaldson, L. G.	2956	Clark, F. C.	3012	Rogers, H. G.
2898	Herbert, W. R.	2957	Levinson, F. C.		
2899	Hewitt, J. R.	2958	Davies, A.	**May, 1943.**	
2900	Hastings, E. E.	2959	Jones, H. J.	3013	Holland, S. H.
2901	White, S. E.	2960	Batten, H. W.	3014	Cook, F. W.
2902	Egalton, W. R.	2961	Miles, B. W.	3015	Williams, F. P.
2903	Jeffery, R. S.	2962	Burbridge, A. F.	3016	Butler, E. E.
2904	Harding, A. W.	2963	Roseberry, A.	3017	Burton, G.
2905	Welch, T. C.	2964	Freaks, T.	3018	Daniel, H. W.
2906	Parker, A. W.			3019	Lawrence, J. A.
2907	Johnson, E. A.	**April, 1943.**		3020	Seccombe, E. C.
2908	Harding, K. E.	2965	Worrall, L. C.	3021	Lee, E. L.
2909	Klapper, C. F.	2966	Graty, J. S.	3022	Law, F.
2910	Everton, R. F.	2967	Haime, F. E.	3023	Laine, A. P.
2911	Hawker, G. F.	2968	Brett, M. L.	3024	Napier, R. S.
2912	Taylor, G. R.	2969	Hoeltchi, G. E.	3025	Kinna, A.
2913	Cork, T. E.	2970	Potter, V. C.	3026	Sanders, P. P.
2914	Hughes, G. F.	2971	Swanson, C. G.	3027	Wilkes, T. F.
2915	Farrell, B. J.	2972	Brown, V. E.	3028	Edey, J.
2916	Holland, J. A. C.	2973	Marshall, V. G.	3029	Purvis, C. G.
2917	Smith, D.	2974	Smith, R. R.	3030	Peel, H. I. F.
2918	Griffin, E. F.	2975	Freeman, H. T.	3031	Waller, E. A.
2919	Quilter, K. M.	2976	Nash, K.	3032	Huggins, R.
2920	Suckling, W. H.	2977	Follett, E. P.	3033	Anderson, J. A.
2921	Harrild, S. G.	2978	Idle, A. E.	3034	Butler, A. E.
2922	Hubbard, W. R.	2979	Clark, E. E.	3035	Mackie, D.
2923	Horwood, J. A. W.	2980	Blanchard, G. W.	3036	Salvage, C. J.
2924	Hardy, K. G.	2981	Hallett, A. E.	3037	May, L. G.
2925	Goddard, H. F.	2982	Howley, E. A.	3038	Hannaford, A. E.
2926	Mauchan, M.	2983	Harris, H.	3039	Willcox, C. E.
2927	Hoad, L. C.	2984	Hobbs, A.	3040	Lee, B.
2928	Read, F. J.	2985	Payne, S. W. J.	3041	Matthews, S. R.
2929	Potter, S. W. M.	2986	Elliott, F.	3042	Ford, G. F.
2930	Head, P. S.	2987	Merrell, D. C.	3043	Dunn, E. A.
2931	Evans, G. B.	2988	Puplett, E. G.	3044	Barrett. W. J.
2932	Brett, F. T.	2989	Dymond, C. R.		
2933	Coton, T.	2990	Plowman, G.	**June, 1943.**	
2934	Hoare, G.	2991	Downing, E. J.	3045	Lavender, S.
2935	Gorbould, C.	2992	Kiely, R. J.	3046	Hodges, F. L.
2936	Hayes, W.	2993	Ruston, P. E.	3047	Arlow, W. L.
2937	Jones, T. G.	2994	Hills, F. J.	3048	Kendall, R. W.
2938	Gillett, J. G.	2995	Roberts, A. G.	3049	Marmon, G. H. F.
2939	Hinz, L.	2996	Hopkins, S. R.	3050	Lowe, J. R.
2940	Ayres, R. O.	2997	Gammon, A. W.	3051	Monk, A. R.
2941	Philpott, F. S.	2998	Moore, R. D.	3052	Miller, B.
2942	Humphrey, E. J.	2999	Sheppard, W. R.	3053	Lilly, H. G.
2943	Hook, V.	3000	Scudder, A. E.	3054	Mitchell, W. G.
2944	Dunning, B. C.	3001	Haffenden, A. E.	3055	Hill, H. D.
2945	Hastings, E. A.	3002	Humphries,	3056	Wise, K. L.
2946	Bluett, I. B. D.		W. E. C.	3057	Goodwin, W. S.
2947	Hopkins, G.	3003	Lewis, S. J.	3058	Town, R. E.

No.	Name	No.	Name	No.	Name
3059	Stead, P. D.	3114	Smith, A. T.	3167	Davies, W. M.
3060	Grubb, C. B.	3115	May, J. A.	3168	Murray, W.
3061	Hider, J.	3116	Patterson, V.	3169	Morgan, G. E. L.
3062	Newton, H. W. G.	3117	Rendell, A.	3170	Trive, C. W.
3063	Miles, P. A.	3118	Busby, P. J.	3171	Warren, F. W.
3064	Mitchell, L. C.	3119	Dunn, L.	3172	Watson, F. C.
3065	Hardwick, D.	3120	Povey, E. W.	3173	Vickers, D. J.
3066	Mummery, A. E.	3121	Wade-Rose, H. C.	3174	Dawe, E. G.
3067	Newman, A. F.	3122	Smith, A. F.	3175	Sadler, E. P.
3068	Thompson, C. C.	3123	Rowland, G. C	3176	Donovan, P. H.
3069	Collard, C. F.	3124	Gadd, H. L.	3177	Rayner, K.
3070	Parish, A. A.	3125	Curtis, P.	3178	Thacker, P. S.
3071	Heather, M. R.	3126	Hawkins, S. S.	3179	Whitehead, J. H.
3072	Frooms, V. H.	3127	Wilton, G. H.	3180	Basham, J. A.
				3181	Webster, A. W.

July, 1943.

3073	Shillingford, R. S.		**September, 1943.**		**November, 1943.**
3074	Martin, A. E.	3128	Hall, T. F.	3182	Speed, J. D. R.
3075	Ashdown, T. E.	3129	Wood, P. E. H.	3183	Jones, G. T.
3076	Topping, C. G.	3130	Fitgerald, E.	3184	Woodley, T. G.
3077	Harvey, C.	3131	Chapman, C. W.	3185	Speich, J. H.
3078	Hawkes, E. T.	3132	Hollingsworth, K.	3186	Collins, M. F. Y.
3079	Boulton, R. S.	3133	Forsdick, J. A.	3187	Beets, W. G.
3080	Hine, S. C.	3134	Coupland, A. E.	3188	Williams, H.
3081	Searchfield, E. R.	3135	Washer, T. A.	3189	Wilby, E. A.
3082	Thomas, J. E.	3136	Boxall, T.	3190	Green, T.
3083	Grubb, F. E.	3137	Sadler, A. G.	3191	Johnsen, R. O. C.
3084	Carter, H. T.	3138	Saberi, P. L.	3192	Boulton, R.
3085	Ovenden, L.	3139	Mungeam, L.	3193	Coleman, J. W.
3086	Blakeman, G. S.	3140	Smith, W. T.	3194	Radlett, W. F.
3087	Robson, H.	3141	Tennant, W. C.	3195	Townsend, E.
3088	Young, R. C.	3142	Tipping, C. W.	3196	Bray, A. D.
3089	Treeton, A. B.	3143	Willett, A.	3197	Piller, T. R.
3090	Humphrey, J. W.	3144	Lacey, C. F.	3198	Sealey, F.
3091	Loxdale, H. A. R.	3145	Price, C.	3199	Luckhurst, A. E.
3092	Poll, E. S. S.	3146	Bostock-Wilson, E. L.	3200	Isard, J. O.
3093	Lynch, H. A.			3201	Yolland, E. R.
3094	Church, W. J. L.	3147	Kentell, S. C.	3202	Dyer, E. A.
3095	Palmer, M. F.	3148	Kemp, R. D.	3203	Copson, H. T.
9096	Poole, E. G. A.	3149	Word, E. E.	3204	Reynolds, T. H.
3097	Silvester, K.	3150	Andrews, J.	3205	Snelling, G. H.
3098	Earney, G. W.	3151	Walsham, J. H.	3206	Philbrick, H. A.
3099	Revill, C. F.	3152	Iremonger, J.	3207	Walsh, D.
3100	Stephens, W. G.	3153	Gould, A. W.	3208	Lambert, A. W.
		3154	Evans, D. W.	3209	Warren, H. H.
	August, 1943.	3155	Perkins, W. H. E.	3210	McEwan, R. H.
3101	Mulholland, A. F.			3211	Coulson, S. A. H.
3102	Santler, S. C.		**October, 1943.**	3212	Monk, W. F.
3103	Johnson, A. W.	3156	Meers, C. P.	3213	Elsworth, J. T.
3104	Wattenbach, J. R.	3157	Philcox, C. R.	3214	Lowe, F. J.
3105	Dwyer, P. J.	3158	Hartmann, W.	3215	Hones, C. F.
3106	Harlow, H. J.	3159	Syms, A. J.	3216	Khong, K. Y.
3107	Holland, K. G.	3160	Dorsett, L. E.	3217	Ruben, C. M.
3108	Janes, R. A.	3161	Brookhouse, A. W	3218	Lemberger, A.
3109	Farrance, W. H. A.	3162	Lee, N.	3219	New, F.
3110	Proctor, L. C.	3163	Bird, H. C.	3220	Burrett, J. H.
3111	Boxall, B. H.	3164	Wilton, D. H.	3221	Morrison, P. J.
3112	Campbell, S. G.	3165	Stone, A. M.	3222	Seal, G.
3113	Grover, R. G.	3166	Lunn, R. M.	3223	Bell, R. S.

No.	Name	No.	Name	No.	Name
December, 1943.		**March, 1944.**		3329	Coxall, J. D.
3224	Lee, E. H. J.	3276	Bethell, J.	3330	Johnston, D. B.
3225	Kennings, W. D.	3277	Sivier, W. S.	3331	Bicknell, F. E.
3226	Harris, R. F.	3278	Headicar, R. J.	3332	Nagle, W. H.
3227	Tweddle, J. H.	3279	Lee, T.	3333	Maloney, J. P.
3228	Clarke, T. H.	3280	Catmur, D. S.	3334	Hughes, C.
3229	Gribble, A. S.	3281	Fisher, E.	3335	Hill, R. J.
3230	Kelly, C. P.	3282	Smith, K. N. S.	3336	Howson, T. M.
		3283	Noore, H. T.	3337	Underhill, R.
January, 1944.		3284	Harding, T. J.	3338	Ruddick, F. F. A.
3231	Payne, F. E.	3285	Baines, R.	3339	Weeks, V. D.
3232	Crawley, A. L.	3286	Craker, P. J.	3340	Motyer, K. A. D.
3233	Summerfield,	3287	Hiley, F.	3341	Priest, A. A. W.
	H. A. E.	3288	Wigan, M. P.	3342	Hamon, E. K.
3234	Walker, R. W.	3289	Anderson, L. D.	3343	Prince, T. H.
3235	Thompson, R.	3290	Parnell, W. F.	3344	Austin, C. A.
3236	Whitehead, S. G.	3291	Cockerton, F. W.	3345	Green, R. A.
3237	Payne, H.	3292	Mercer, C. T.	3346	Fairclough, E. J.
3238	Allen, J. E.	3293	Chapman, A. J.	3347	Taylor, K. A.
3239	Bailey, S.	3294	Newman, A. J.	3348	Jordan, T. A.
3240	Harding, E.	3295	Singfield, G. D.	3349	Callow, R. R.
3241	Marchant, H. S.	3296	Watson, F. S. B.	3350	Gusselle, A. A.
3242	Game, A. E.	3297	Jones, C. E.	3351	Steplehurst, J. S.
3243	Reeves, G. F.	3298	Duddy, G. E.	3352	Lankenau, G. J. S
3244	Daley, G. F.			3353	Wright, W. R.
3245	Vince, H. B.	**April, 1944.**		3354	Wordley, R.
3246	Kallmeir, F.	3299	Steer, G. V.	3355	Champion, G. W
3247	May, J. K.	3300	Ballinger, W. R.	3356	Batten, D. F.
3248	Warren, M. D.	3301	Dowding, C. H.	3357	Worrill, H.
3249	Gowar, A. D. H.	3302	Miller-Brown,	3358	Ingles, R. H.
3250	Clark, P. W.		C. E.	3359	Milner, R. H.
3251	Willis, W. R.	3303	Andrews, B. W.	3360	Spears, J. R.
3252	Marlow, W. J.	3304	Lindars, L. W.	3361	Wilson, J.
3253	Filose, E. J.	3305	Aeberhard, A.	3362	Stubbings, N. D.
3254	Dudley, C. H.	3306	Clarke, P. F.	3363	Tilley, J. E.
3255	Barton, J. E.	3307	Hunt, J.	3364	Ingles, F. W.
3256	Robinson, W. W.	3308	Livett, L. J.	3365	Macey, J. E. E.
3257	Misslebrook, C. J.	3309	Richards, F. C.	3366	Relton, H.
3258	Smith, A. S.	3310	Roser, A. E.	3367	Smart, J. W.
3259	Kinnear, J. A. C.	3311	Ling, H. J.	3368	Gooch, D. S. J.
3260	Osborne, E.	3312	Baker, L. S. H.	3369	Clements, S. H.
3261	Schoenberg,	3313	Speller, F. V.	3370	Smith, L. A.
	F. A. G.	3314	Carter, A. G.	3371	Dwyer, H. E. G.
3262	Vandy, G. E.	3315	Horst, H. E.	3372	Killey, E.
		3316	Hughes, A. C.	3373	Harrison, D.
February, 1944.		3317	Bond, H. F.	3374	Aylward, G. P.
3263	Shackleford, E. W.	3318	Cohen, M.	3375	Miller, G.
3264	Day, W. H.	3319	Laraman, C. J. N.	3376	Popham, L. A.
3265	Imeson, F. G.	3320	Crowhurst, W. J.	3377	Sayers, R. A. V.
3266	Bacque, D. W. P.	3321	Meyer, H. J.	3378	Humphris, J. N.
3267	Bassett, R. W.	3322	Thompson, V. G.	3379	Kendall, I. R.
3268	Wimbush, J. W.	3323	Coe, H. T.	3380	Smith, J. A.
3269	Bayliss, H. J.	3324	Smith, J.	3381	Martin, W. D.
3270	Noakes, F. D. L.				
3271	Pedlar, E. J.	**May, 1944.**		**June, 1944.**	
3272	Wicks, A. L.	3325	Bishop, G. W.	3382	Griffin, J. C.
3273	Stone, R. G.	3326	Hibbert, L. E.	3383	Carlton, E. J.
3274	Welbrook, A. H.	3327	Dunford, B. J.	3384	Dwyer, D. A.
3275	Griffiths, M. S.	3328	Howson, D. T.	3385	Young, R.

No.	Name	No.	Name	No.	Name
3386	Hayles, P. D.	3398	Williams, A. J.	3410	Findley, J.
3387	Panther, J. B.	3399	Edwards, A.	3411	Jackson, J.
3388	Atterton, W. V.	3400	Wooder, R. A.	3412	Kindred, W. A.
3389	Leppenwell, J. E.	3401	Dunne, E.	3413	Duddy, G. E.
3390	Weeks, W. G.	3402	Bournat, A. C.	3414	Hearn, R. J.
3391	Westcott, W. G.	3403	Starr, H. H.	3415	Jurn, A. J.
3392	Forder, B. A.	3404	Earl, A.	3416	Elliott, F.
3393	Wallace, C. G.	3405	Russell, S. K.	3417	Harris, A. G.
3394	Francis, A. J.	3406	Thornton, A.	3418	Ditton, J. O.
3395	Ghost, W. T.	3407	Gardner, G. D.	3419	Gilder, S. G.
3396	Lavender, L. A.	3408	Mansfield, D..D.	3420	Collins, D. C.
3397	Brosnon, C. R.	3409	Jones, E. A.		

ELECTRICITY UNIT

No.	Name	No.	Name	No.	Name
ED 1	Trend, W. G.	ED29	Davies, H. J.	ED57	Dennett, A. W.
ED 2	Scott, E. R.	ED30	Abrehart, C.	ED58	Barrow, F.
ED 3	Collins, W. J.	ED31	Paffett, B.	ED59	Rose, S.
ED 4	McGill, A. G.	ED32	Simmonds, T.	ED60	Stenning, C.
ED 4A	Costin, E. W.	ED32A	Sadler, S.	ED61	Grieve, S.
ED 5	Curwood, D.	ED33	Lettington, S.	ED61A	Rawlings, F.
ED 6	Hider, J.	ED34	Perry, W.	ED62	Morris, W. R.
ED 6A	Sharman, J.	ED35	Mobbs, R.	ED63	Richards, L. W.
ED 6B	Storey, G.	ED96	Stone, W. T.	ED69A	Fuller, R. C.
ED 7	Weeks, R.	ED97	Ovenden, S.	ED64	Hale, F.
ED 8	Gurr, H.	ED97A	Avis, L. A.	ED65	Pyke, W.
ED 9	Elliott, R.	ED38	Page, A. C.	ED66	Banham, A.
ED10	Gauntlett, S.	ED39	Yearley, C.	ED67	Davies, G. D.
ED11	Wyatt, H.	ED40	Coveney, P. H.	ED67A	Staples, J.
ED12	Moy, P.	ED40A	Stears, W. A.	ED68	Davies, H. G.
ED13	Bax, C. W.	ED40B	Austin, W. H.	ED69	Davies, L.
ED14	Perry, F.	ED41	Davies, R.	ED70	May, C. L.
ED15	Boxall, A.	ED42	Baynton, A. W.	ED71	Sims, C.
ED16	Brigden, W.	ED43	Dent, E.	ED72	Smith, T.
ED17	Jones, J.	ED44	Coulter, F.	ED73	Walker, G.
ED18	Gardner, S.	ED45	Bradshaw, A. J.	ED74	Turner, A.
ED19	Ashdown, T.	ED46	Collins, F.	ED74A	Warwick, F.
ED20	Murphy, J.	ED46A	Brown, J.	ED75	Smith, E. S.
ED20A	Philpot, A.	ED47	Reeves, H.	ED75A	Winn, D.
ED21	Armstrong, H.	ED48	Paine, N.	ED76	Ward, K.
ED22	Distill, H.	ED49	Reid, P.	ED76A	Trend, D.
ED22A	McGlone, C. M.	ED50	Collins, G.	ED77	Mallett, F. J.
ED23	Douglas, W.	ED51	Ward, W.	ED78	Smith, W. A.
ED24	Laar, L.	ED52	Taylor, A.	ED79	Kingston, C.
ED25	Ashton, A. H.	ED53	Scarborough, C.	ED80	Wood, E. V.
ED26	Clark, G.	ED54	Wade, F.	ED81	Mitchell, R.
ED27	Lettington, H.	ED55	Bateman, H.		
ED28	Friend, B.	ED56	Dyer, E. A.		

WOMEN AUXILIARIES

No.	Name
May, 1943.	
Woodrow, Miss J.	
Kind, Mrs. F. M.	
June, 1943.	
Stunden, Miss E. M.	
Woodward, Miss E. F.	
Sawyer, Miss M. E.	
Church, Mrs. F. A.	
Harris, Mrs. N. B.	
Rackham, Mrs. E. D.	
Porter, Mrs. E. M.	
Mercer, Miss N. R. C.	
Morgan, Miss W.	
Chance, Mrs. E. N.	
Sutton, Mrs. D. W.	
Carter, Mrs. E. M.	
Carter, Miss B. M.	
White, Miss L.	

No.	Name
Shergold, Mrs. S. A. E.	
Thomas, Mrs. N. B.	
Filby, Mrs. E. M.	
Payn, Miss D.	
July, 1943.	
Pitkin, Miss E. M.	
Waas, Miss G. E.	
Clark, Mrs. M.	
Day, Mrs. W. L.	
Gidley, Mrs. L. L.	
Broughton, Mrs. F.	
Tremble, Mrs. M. E.	
Williams, Mrs. A. E.	
Leach, Mrs. M.	
Smith, Mrs. D. F.	
Moran, Mrs. G. D.	

No.	Name
August, 1943.	
Ransley, Mrs. E. R.	
Hill, Mrs. A. G.	
Young, Miss S. M.	
Wells, Miss D.	
Gardner, Miss M. E.	
September, 1943.	
Beets, Mrs. R. A.	
Mansell, Miss D.	
Payne, Mrs. D.	
Loder, Mrs. E. F.	
May, 1944.	
Frost, Miss J. M.	
June, 1944.	
Sanderson, Mrs. P. K.	
Lever, Miss J. P.	

Nominal Roll of Members of the Battalion who have joined the Services

Abbreviations :

R.N.	=	Royal Navy
R.M.	=	Royal Marines
R.A.F.	=	Royal Air Force
M.N.	=	Merchant Navy

No.	Name	Branch of Service	No.	Name	Branch of Service
A COMPANY			2463	Goodsman, E.	Army
1895	Andrews, D. H.	Army	1389	Groom, C. J. .	Army
808	Aldcroft, K.	M.N.	1982	Goulding, A. G.	Army
1135	Brown, H.	R.N.	2950	Head, P. E.	Army
1320	Bartlett, A. C. .	Army	681	Harper, R. A.	Army
1400	Bloomfield, A. E.	Army	812	Hartman, T. B.	Army
1449	Bond, G. A. A.	R.A.F.	1555	Hopper, A. F.	Army
342	Brooke, D. .	Army	1343	Haisman, H. B.	Army
1930	Broucke, H. P.	Belgian Army	1872	Harman, E. W. .	Army
2630	Buckland, F. W.	Army	2254	Henning, G. W. T.	R.N.
659	Butcher, C. F.	R.A.F.	2562	Halfpenny, J. T.	Army
1792	Bromley, G. O.	Army	2994	Hills, E. J. ..	Army
901	Batchelor, F. G.	R.N.	2895	Jameson, H.	R.N.
1202	Barclay, F. . .	Army	1288	Jeffs, P. G.	Army
1825	Burtenshaw, L. A. .	Army	2057	Jones, N. J. .	R.N.
1826	Burtenshaw, C. J.	Army	2687	Kensington, J. M.	Army
1349	Baker, L. C. J.	Army	1793	Kingston, C. H.	Army
2834	Baker, B. L.	Army	2418	Kemp, D. .	Army
815	Croucher, B. R.	R.A.F.	651	Lyddiard, W. T.	Army
17	Clarke, W. H.	Army	2165	Latham, C. R.	Army
2163	Catlett, C. V.	Army	2044	Lloyd, R. D.	Army
2358	Capel, W. J.	Army	2253	Leach, W. J. . .	Army
116	Coulson, A. G. .	Army	382	Mountfort, L. T. W.	Army
1847	Cowell, C. P.	Army	861	Muirhead, J.	Army
2438	Carse, J. O.	Army	952	Martin, E. T.	Army
2768	Cox, P. H. . .	Army	1762	Morley, A. T.	R.N.
3211	Coulson, S. A. H.	Army	2391	Nevett, F. J.	R.N.
1141	Cobley, A. P. M.	R.A.F.	1001	Ovens, S. A.	Army
1230	Collins, J. T.	R.A.F.	1033	Ovens, A. L.	Army
1893	Cardinal, S. W.	R.N.	1106	Price, A. .	Army
1965	Comport, A. L.	Army	1426	Pollard, L. W.	Army
2011	Carver, D. W.	Army	2988	Puplett, E. G.	R.N.
1163	Day, C. . .	Army	940	Phillips, F. B.	Army
1026	Derbyshire, E. C. . .	Army	950	Pickard, C. C.	R.A.F.
2030	De Gier, P. R.	Dutch Army	1863	Riley, M. A.	R.M.
843	Dixon, G. E. B.	R.N.	1812	Robinson, C. H.	R.A.F.
1280	Dennis, W.	Army	1798	Rawson, A. F.	Army
2262	Eastcott, D. W.	R.A.F.	2212	Suttie, W. J.	Army
2054	Golding, W.	Army	1097	Smith, C. .	R.N.
899	Giles, E.	Army	1204	Smith, D. A. G.	Army

No.	Name	Branch of Service	No.	Name	Branch of Service
2200	Savage, R. A. E.	R.N.	1351	Smedley, D.	R.A.F.
1840	Sherwin, K. E.	Army	1596	Stevens, G. D. .	R.N.
1834	Sturgeon, R. H.	Army	1387	Smith, N. H.	R.N.
1165	Sherwood, R. F.	Army	2733	Sievewright, R.	R.N.
2737	Sims, L. C. .	Army	1108	Smith, F.	R.A.F.
196	Thomas, W.	R.A.F.	1543	Sales, J. .	Army
2369	Tilzey, G. .	R.N.	844	Tabor, O. H.	R.N.
1782	Trigg, G. H.	Army	1687	Tebbutt, J. R.	Army
2406	Wilshaw, J.	Army	1606	Tidbury, A.	Army
820	Wise, G. G.	R.N.	655	Vink, H. K.	R.A.F.
2777	Walsh, F. C.	R.N.	1453	Wright, W. J.	R.N.
1119	Zealey, W. J.	R.A.F.	968	Williams, G.	R.A.F.
			1732	Windett, F. .	Army
B COMPANY			768	Windsor, H. A. L. .	R.A.F.
937	Austin, A. E.	R.A.			
1611	Allchin, G. T.	Army	**C COMPANY**		
2301	Bodiam, G. H. .	R.N.	1999	Alexander, C. G.	R.N.
1078	Boakes, H. H.	R.M.	1630	Arbon, H. G.	R.A.F.
2727	Bowditch, P. S.	Army	2144	Archer, R. .	R.M.
379	Boxshall, C. C. W.	Army	924	Arnold, A. W. . .	R.A.F.
756	Bass, B. W. . , .	Army	2413	Arrowsmith, A. W.	R.A.F.
1297	Brunner, L. W.	Army	317	Ashlee, F. P. .	Army
1200	Cheshire, D. A.	Army	2478	Babbage, C. W.	Army
798	Coomber, A. J.	Army	763	Barnes, J. T.	R.A.F.
2099	Cooper, G. W. S.	R.A.F.	733	Beadle, J. A.	Army
663	Crouch, F. W.	R.A.F.	1089	Bennett, R. W.	R.A.F.
1206	Cox, E. C.	Army	1527	Bishop, D. G.	R.A.F.
1690	Cross, T. F.	Army	2946	Bluett, I. B. D.	Army
726	Gale, G. A.	Army	2394	Boswell, A. L.	R.A.F.
743	Gordon, F. W. ,	Army	2033	Boyd, I. M.	R.N.
764	Gorton, F. F.	Army	832	Bridges, A. R.	Army
1629	Gooch, J. C.	Army	1221	Britton, A.	R.A.F.
1136	Hall, S. R. .	Army	1636	Brown, L. . .	R.N.
1537	Higgs, D. F.	Army	1238	Buckingham, C.	Army
2664	Harrod, P. . . .	Army	1943	Bumstead, F.	Army
637	Hunter, J. A. de C.	Army	582	Bullen, W. H. .	Army
668	Hunt, J. S. M. .	R.A.F.	1576	Burbridge, E. A.	Army
1873	Holden, E. J.	R.N.	1380	Burbidge, T. G. .	R.N.
728	Hollick, F. . .	Army	1471	Burningham, H. W.	R.A.F.
1725	Jennings, G. H.	Army	685	Catmur, R. E.	R.N.
585	James, F. C.	R.N.	2476	Chantell, G. H. .	R.N.
1329	Johnson, H. E. .	Army	545	Christopherson, G. R. .	R.A.F.
1705	Jones, R. D.	R.A.F.	1518	Churchett, F. N.	R.A.F.
765	Knopp, B. B.	Army	619	Clegg, G. R.	Army
1634	Kirk, H. L.	Army	1565	Clouder, A. E.	Army
1817	Kennedy, S. P.	R.A.F.	1344	Collis, G. A.	R.N.
1985	Moore, W. M.	Army	1069	Coltman, K. A. S. .	R.A.F.
2326	Mitchell, E. W.	R.N.	954	Constant, K. L.	Army
1768	Mead, A. E.	Army	2422	Cook, R. A.	Army
1862	Neal, D. J. . .	R.A.F.	2775	Cook, D.	Army
2274	Norton, P. G. M.	Army	562	Cowburn, K. J.	R.A.F.
1138	Page, J. A. .	Army	2437	Cope, M. V.	Army
1485	Parker, R. A.	R.A.F.	961	Dabner, K. C.	R.N.
1502	Patty, F. .	R.N.	2633	Dadd, R. A.	Army
2067	Patient, T. C.	M.N.	838	Dangerfield, C. C. .	R.A.F.
1964	Preece, J. .	R.N.	2375	Dann, H. J.	Army
1868	Roberts, C. J.	Army	2066	Davids, P. H.	R.N.
985	Sayers, J.	R.A.F.	1919	Davis, P. A.	R.A.F

[73]

No.	Name	Branch of Service
1885	Way, A. W.	R.N.
2344	Whitnell, J.	M.N.
955	Whitehouse, D. F. .	Army
543	Wickham, J.	Army
911	Williams, H.	R.N.
2133	Williams, R. A.	R.A.F.
467	Williamson, G. E.	R.N.
1099	Winslade, G. S.	R.A.F.
2435	Winter, J. A. V.	Army
1038	Wisdom, C. A. .	Army
1164	Wright, W. F.	M.N.

D COMPANY

No.	Name	Branch of Service
957	Acton, G. E. .	R.A.F.
2718	Anderson, B. R.	R.N.
2940	Ayres, R. O.	R.A.F.
2079	Bagshaw, W. S.	R.A.F.
1353	Ball, S. J. .	Army
1046	Bassam, R. A. .	Army
1683	Benham, G. W.	Army
1688	Bratton, D.	Army
269	Brodie, R. .	Army
1259	Brookes, R. H. .	R.A.F.
156	Brown, L. S.	R.N.
1297	Brunner, L. W.	Army
2872	Carter, E. G.	Army
2250	Chandler, S. T.	R.N.
1742	Clare, E. G. G.	Army
1150	Clark, R. V.	Army
2724	Collins, T. J.	Army
1761	Cook, A. . .	Army
1257	Crowhurst, R. F.	R.N.
866	Cruttenden, H. S.	R.A.F.
1955	Debbonaire, J. S.	R.N.
1937	Doughty, J. A. .	Army
2139	Dray, F. T. S.	Army
1336	Drew, H. G.	Army
2099	Drew, M. .	Army
517	Easton, D. H.	Army
2472	Edmeads, L. R.	R.N.
1040	Eglington, E.	R.A.F.
682	Everest, R. E.	Army
688	Ferris, S. J. .	R.A.F.
1546	Ford, R. E.	Army
518	Garcia, R. A.	Army
1192	Gibbs, S. W.	Army
940	Gilliard, E. A.	Army
1914	Gleeson, M. E.	Army
2876	Greenway, W.	Army
1838	Gregory, G. J. .	Army
2856	Gregory, W. H.	R.N.
2471	Grimshaw, J. A.	Army
1110	Harding, H. J. .	Army
1909	Harvey, J. S. A.	M.N.
1497	Hastings, L. J.	Army
2127	Hills, S. .	Mines
1171	Hodgson, L. E.	R.A.F.
1822	Humphries, M.	Army

No.	Name	Branch of Service
2130	Jeffery, R. W.	Army
2192	Jones, E. M.	Army
2514	Joyce, K. D.	Army
528	Joyce, R. W. .	R.A.F.
892	Judge, C. L. W.	R.A.F.
2052	Knight, R. C.	R.N.
962	Love, C. B. .	R.A.F.
2034	Mabbs, C. P.	R.N.
1728	Martin, E. .	Army
880	Mayhew, D. J. .	R.N.
592	McCree, W.	Army
1441	McCullagh, H.	R.A.F.
1282	Miles, C. P.	R.N.
1534	Miles, B, W.	Army
1424	Milton, D. G.	Army
1385	Moreley, B. T.	R.A.F.
932	Morgan, R. H.	R.A.F.
1797	Monks, R. W. M.	R.A.F.
2137	Paffett, L. J. .	R.N.
729	Paine, B. G.	R.A.F.
2906	Parker, A. W.	R.N.
758	Parker, E. .	Army.
725	Parker, S. E.	R.N.
1760	Pearson, A. H.	R.N.
476	Ponsford, R.	R.A.F.
1910	Powell, D. A.	R.M.
1848	Powell, P. J.	R.A.F.
1239	Reeves, N. P.	Army
1084	Reynolds, L.	Army
926	Sayers, L. R.	R.A.F.
2469	Sayers, R. . .	Army
868	Sayers, T. E. G.	R.A.F.
1122	Seton, R. C.	Army
1655	Skinner, W.	Army
464	Smith, F. J.	R.A.F.
1511	Smith, J.	Army
440	Spicer, F. C.	Army
2355	Startup, W. D.	Army
1766	Sullivan, D. D.	M.N.
1452	Tamlyn, B. A.	R.A.F.
1281	Terry, R. G. .	R.N.
3068	Thompson, C. C.	R.N.
1472	Thorpe, G. H.	R.A.F.
736	Towell, A. C.	R.A.F.
155	Troquet, P. C.	Army
1744	Troubridge, H. G.	R.N.
1299	Twomey, R. E.	R.A.F.
1250	Wakelin, J. .	Army
2117	Walker, A. A.	R.A.F.
1283	Waters, R. A.	R.A.F.
1113	Weatherall, S. A.	Army
951	White, R. A.	R.A.F.
2164	Willson, W. H.	Army
2815	Wilson, N. A.	Army
3127	Wilton, G. W.	Army

M.G. COMPANY

No.	Name	Branch of Service
1966	Attwood, A. J.	Army

No.	Name	Branch of Service	No.	Name	Branch of Service
969	Andrews, D. J. T.	Army	1010	Freakes, R. A. M.	R.A.F.
1216	Adams, R. R. D.	Army	1851	Gregory, D. W.	R.N.
1820	Brady, F. S.	Army	1961	Gale, S. E. . .	Army
2458	Ball, F. J.	R.N.	1326	Gentle, H. W. J. . .	R.A.F.
953	Ball, R. J.	Army	1784	Gregory, G. J. . . ◢	R.N.
1656	Barlow, J.	Army	1646	Guildford, E. T. G.	Army
2294	Basham, E. .	Army	1324	Gentle, H. H.-	R.A.F.
1945	Bathe, S. M.	Army	1087	Gilham, C. C.	R.N.
2615	Bauch, E. . .	Army	989	Hall, D. H.	Army
1466	Berryman, H. W.	R.N.	1130	Hallford, A.	Army
2680	Biggar, A. D. .	R.N.	1972	Hardy, C. A.	R.N.
1059	Biggenden, G. W.	R.N.	1301	Hayter, D. E.	Army
2531	Binder, R. H.	Army	869	Hewitt, D. C.	R.A.F.
1242	Bloss, R. G.	R.M.	1120	Hicks, T. A.	R.A.F.
1359	Bogen, G. A.	Army	1735	Higgins, R. . .	R.N.
1756	Bowden, E. F.	R.N.	2186	Hilder, E. C. H.	Army
1160	Brady, J. T.	Army	1971	Hopkins, L. C. M.	R.N.
2223	Brain, A. E.	Army	2217	Hough, H. G.	Army
1731	Brooker, W.	Army	1478	Howe, W. R. .	R.N.
2651	Burt, A. E.	Army	1342	Haslewood, A. C.	R.N.
1720	Baker, R. F.	Army	1031	Hirst, H. E. .	R.A.F.
1112	Brady, W. J.	Army	980	Hainsworth, E. C. .	R.A.F.
1891	Bennett; F.	Army	1598	Horsey, W. S.	Army
1148	Berriman, B.	R.N.	2140	Inwood, D. R.	R.N.
1906	Bates, D.	R.N.	2861	Jenner, A. J.	Army
1327	Brown, J. A.	Army	1764	King, G. W. .	R.A.F.
1284	Bayes, W. .	Army	1005	Lansbury, E. R.	Army
1757	Bax, D. R. C.	Army	2031	Lawrence, D. L.	Army
1509	Carman, G. J.	R.N.	1211	Ledger, P. G.	R.N.
2473	Carr, C. F.	R.N.	1603	Livermore, R. .	R.A.F.
1781	Carter, A. K.	R.N.	1361	Lovell, E. H. V.	Army
1151	Colvin, K. J.	R.N.	1934	Maddison, G. .	R.N.
2410	Cook, T. J. .	Army	1552	Marriott, M. V.	R.A.F.
2672	Corley, W.	Army	1803	Mason, C.	Army
1852	Cox, L. R. . .	R.N.	1213	May, E. C. .	Army
1578	Crossman, G. E.	R.A.F.	1152	McCalla, K. V.	Army
1008	Cook, P. V.	R.A.F.	2120	Merrett, E. C.	R.N.
1060	Cock, P. K.	Army	1959	Moore, P. W.	Army
1124	Cowling, P. R. .	R.A.F.	1115	Maskens, D. F. . .	Army
1394	Campbell, I. M. .	R.N.	1510	McNaughton, S. R. M.	Army
1482	Crowhurst, E. H. G.	Army	1322	Mann, L. E. .	R.N.
1599	Chick, H. J.	R.N.	1461	McClory, D. O'D.	R.A.F.
2121	Daniels, A.	Army	1685	Morter, W. F.	R.A.F.
1360	Davey, W. A.	R.A.F.	1861	Nutkins, P. A. .	Army
1704	Dixon, W. A.	Army	1346	Newman, R. R.	Army
1633	Doubleday, E.	R.A.F.	1579	Nichols, G. H.	Army
1347	Deason, R. S.	R.A.F.	988	Olivo, O. .	Army
1622	Dalley, O. J.	Army	1179	O'Brien, H. P.	R.A.F.
1878	Evans, O. E.	R.A.F.	1357	Pascoe, D. J.	Army
1040	Eglington, E.	R.A.F.	2323	Pegram, E.	R.N.
1325	Egleton, R. F. . .	R.N.	2990	Plowman, G. .	R.M.
1460	Edenborough, J. B. D..	R.A.F.	1807	Plummer, E. R.	Army
1722	Edmeades, W. M.	Army	991	Portlock, G. F. .	R.N.
1064	Fleet, K. A.	Army	1431	Potter, D. J. .	R.A.F.
2238	French, E. G. .	Army	1464	Parry, G. W. T.	Army
1456	Fromings, W. R.	R.N.	1913	Quinlan, J. .	Army
1967	Franck, M. L.		2321	Roberts, C. . .	Army
		Free French Navy	1405	Robinson, H. J.	R.N.

No.	Name	Branch of Service	No.	Name	Branch of Service
1181	Rosenthal, P. J.	R.M.	2467	Hull, A. R.	Army
1161	Rottenbury, L. C.	Army	2546	Humphrey, W. A.	Army
1089	Rowe, P. W. V.	R.A.F.	837	Hyde, C. W.	R.A.F.
1642	Russell, L. J.	R.M.	2153	Jameson, R. L.	R.N.
1526	Raper, S. E.	R.N.	732	Janes, S. L. R.	Army
1074	Selby, F.	Army	2251	Jenkin, V. G.	R.A.F.
1892	Smith, R. J.	Army	2240	Kentell, R. C.	Army
1832	Smith, W. J. R.	R.A.F.	3045	Lavender, S.	R.A.F.
1128	Somers, F. W.	R.N.	2062	Lawson, R. E.	Army
1765	Sturgeon, G. W.	Army	1480	Lee, W. C.	R.M.
986	Stickland, D. R.	R.A.F.	1998	Light, D. G.	R.A.F.
1094	Speed, M. J. D.	R.A.F.	824	Mitchell, E. F.	Army
2514	Tanner, C. S.	M.N.	2025	Morgan, W. G.	R.A.F.
977	Tanner, D. R.	R.N.	1055	Nicolle, E. C.	R.N.
1090	Tice, A. E.	Army	1172	Nineham, F. E.	R.A.F.
1401	Towell, N. T.	Army	2043	Norris, R. K.	R.M.
1935	Trueman, W. L.	R.A.F.	1533	Norton, B. D.	R.N.
2004	Turner, C. A.	Army	2242	Nottage, L. W.	Army
1949	Vaile, S. E.	R.N.	2544	Pavey, F. W.	Army
1802	Valentine, L. E.	Army	2064	Pearce, G.	M.N.
2400	Van den Bergh, E. A. R.	R.A.F.	2264	Pike, D. W.	Army
1437	Wedderburn, F. A.	R.A.F.	1695	Plail, J. A.	R.M.
1588	Westwood, W. L.	Army	1916	Punchard, A.	R.M.
1857	Wickenden, G. W.	R.N.	1089	Reynolds, L.	Army
1462	Wilson, A.	Army	2519	Sargeant, H. J.	R.N.
2145	Winwood, R. O.	Army	1355	Scott, R. A. L.	Army
1577	Wood, G. E.	Army	234	Shenton, P.	R.N.
1319	Woodward, F. H.	Army	2505	Shenwood, R. A.	R.A.F.
1082	Williams, T. A.	R.N.	2172	Shurety, P. R.	Army
1058	Watson, D. J. W.	R.A.F.	2591	Sisley, L. J.	Army
1245	Wilkie, A. S.	Army	2571	Stennett, W.	Army
			2273	Stiff, R. A.	Army
MOBILE COLUMN			1294	Taylor, G. D.	Army
2076	Allin, D. I.	Army	2168	Turner, A. G.	M.N.
2104	Avery, M. J.	Army	2949	White, J. T.	R.M.
1268	Beer, K.	R.N.	633	Whybrow, W.	Army
1917	Biggs, A. T.	R.N.	3056	Wise, K. L.	R.N.
2197	Bowen, J. A.	R.A.F.			
2105	Boxall, S. G.	Army	**ELECTRICITY UNIT**		
1228	Burgess, F. R.	Army	37A	Avis, L.	Army
2147	Carrington, H. W.	Army	63A	Fuller, R. C.	R.N.
1833	Clark, M. S.	Army	4	McGill, A. G. D.	R.N.
2159	Clarke, F. E.	Army	76A	Trend, D. J. F.	R.N.
2113	Crowest, T. P.	Army	6A	Sharman, E. V.	R.A.F.
3264	Day, W. H.	Army	67A	Staples, J. S.	R.A.F.
2520	Dempsey, P. G.	Army	40B	Austin, W. H.	R.A.F.
2292	Douglas, A.	Army	42	Baynton, A. W.	Army
1653	Dove, J. M.	R.N.	46A	Brown, J. I.	Army
2327	Drew, W. B.	Army	46	Collins, F.	Army
1791	Elliott, W.	Army	50	Collins, G. E.	M.N.
2964	Freakes, T.	R.N.	68	Davies, H. G. J.	Army
2204	Gregory, C. P.	R.N.	69	Davies, L. H.	R.A.F.
1522	Grinham, R. A.	Army	41	Davies, R. F.	Army
2593	Griscoll, E. W.	M.N.	43	Dent, E. V.	Army
2089	Hancock, F.	R.N.	8	Gurr, H.	R.A.F.
2106	Harris, A. P.	R.N.	64	Hale, F. A.	R.A.F.
2351	Henneker, M. H.	M.N.	6	Hider, J.	Army
3007	Holland, G.	Army	79	Kingston, R. C.	Army

No.	Name	Branch of Service	No.	Name	Branch of Service
33	Lettington, H. M.	Army	1235	Day, D. A.	Army
70	May, C. L.	R.A.F.	884	Dighton, H. J.	Army
20	Murphy, J. D.	M.N.	3119	Dunn, L.	Army
34	Perry, W. H.	Army	1957	Ecott, C. R.	Army
20A	Philpott, W. A.	Army	721	Eyles, G. L.	R.A.F.
65	Pyke, W. H.	R.A.F.	723	Fabry, J. F.	Army
63	Richards, L. W.	R.N.	3109	Farrence, W. H. A.	R.M.
71	Sims, G. E.	Army	1364	Farr, F. F.	R.M.
75	Smith, E. S.	Army	1625	Ford, A. A.	Army
72	Smith, T. E.	M.N.	1620	Fordham, E.	Army
40A	Stears, W. A.	Army	1210	Fox, D. F.	R.N.
6B	Storey, G. F. S.	R.N.	1813	Freeman, H. T.	Army
74	Turner, A. L.	R.N.	1019	Fromings, G.	Army
73	Walker, G.	Army	1883	Fullerton, S. G.	Army
74A	Warwick, F. W.	R.A.F.	1770	Gamm, G. B.	Army
76	Ward, K. G. H.	R.N.	722	Gamm, K. B.	Army
51	Ward, W. T. R.	R.N.	1879	Hadfield, E. G.	Army

HEAVY TRANSPORT SECTION

No.	Name	Branch of Service	No.	Name	Branch of Service
2857	Batchelor, G. W.	Army	708	Hall, P.	Army
2453	Bax, D. R. C.	Army	1756	Hards, C. O.	Army
2460	Beal, R. E.	Army	724	Harvey, K. T.	R.A.F.
2468	Brimmer, R. E.	Army	869	Hewott, D. C.	R.A.F.
1394	Campbell, I. M.	R.N.	2887	John, C. E.	Army
2279	Cooper, L. G.	R.N.	2343	Jones, P. R.	Army
2953	Dudley, A. E.	R.N.	1157	Jordan, K.	R.M.
1775	Everest, D. J.	Army	2715	Kenway, S.	Army
2314	Hall, E. H.	Army	716	Lee, G. H.	R.A.F.
2475	Ham, E. J.	Army	885	Lines, W. J.	Army
1425	Henning, J.	M.N.	1368	Mackintosh, J. A.	R.A.F
757	Higgs, R.	R.A.F.	835	Marriott, A. G.	Army
2674	Kemp, D. B.	Army	2091	Marshal, W. T.	R.A.F.
1005	Lansbury, E. K.	Army	880	Mayhew, D. J.	R.A.F.
2459	Matholie, P.	R.N.	1703	Maynard, K. F.	R.N.
1846	Maynard, A. W.	R.N.	928	Noonan, S.	Army
2176	Meade, E. L.	R.N.	2729	Pearson, J. F.	R.A.F
2118	Meyer, W. F.	Army	717	Potts, D.	R.A.F.
2624	Mitchell, H. M.	Army	3194	Radlett, W. F.	Army
1251	Palin, F.	R.N.	1995	Raiman, H. T.	Army
711	Potts, R.	R.A.F.	887	Robertson, J. P.	Army
717	Potts, D.	Army	3175	Sadler, E. P.	Army
2396	Sparks, G. E. C.	R.N.	709	Sargent, N. A. C.	Army
1796	Stimson, W. E.	R.N.	2173	Scrivens, K.	R.A.F.
2357	Svenson, D. P.	R.N.	811	Segar, J. P.	Army
2567	Wale, K. H.	R.N.	2316	Spears, G. H.	Army
2456	Wallace, F. M.	R.M.	1532	Storey, G.	Army
2384	Waters, C. J. E.	Army	719	Tooke, H. E.	Army
1523	Webb, J. J.	Army	902	Wall, H. E.	Army
1234	Whitaker, R. A.	R.A.F.	883	Wiltshire, D.	Army
2177	Wilson, E. W.	Army			
1992	Wood, K. W.	R.A.F.		BAND	
2393	Worthington, B. S.	R.N.	1697	Barnett, H. C.	R.A.F.
			1597	Calvert, N.	Army

HEADQUARTERS SIG SEC.

No.	Name	Branch of Service	No.	Name	Branch of Service
			1618	Charles, A.	Army
1436	Aldous, D. G.	Army	2455	Ferris, R.	Mines
808	Allcroft, K. D.	M.N.	2301	Hyland, T.	Army
2444	Banks, D. J.	Army	1732	King, W.	R.A.F.
1821	Billings, A. C.	Army	2449	Piper, H.	Army
710	Bruce, H. P.	Army	1616	Simpson, C.	Army
			2138	Wilson, F.	R.N.

List of Officers who served in the Battalion

From February 1, 1942 until Stand Down

Commanding Officer	(a) Lt.-Col. T. ETCHELLS, D.S.O., M.C.
	(b) Lt.-Col. H. W. O'BRIEN, M.C., T.D.
Second-in-Command	(a) Major H. W. O'BRIEN, M.C., T.D.
	(b) Major H. D. REYNOLDS, M.C.
Adjutant .	Capt. F. D. HOYS (Gen. List)
Quartermaster	(a) Capt. V. W. CUNIS (Gen. List)
	(b) Capt. F. G. FRENCH (R.A.)
Weapons Training Officer	(a) Capt. P. S. AYERS, M.C.
	(b) Capt. F. J. BUTCHER
Intelligence Officer	Capt. H. H. PAYNE, M.C.
Medical Officer . . .	Major A. T. ROGERS
Sub-Unit Medical Officers	Capt. W. S. HUNT
	Capt. REX YOLLAND
	Capt. C. DYSART
	Capt. J. H. HOPTON
Musketry Officer	(a) Lt. H. W. WALTER
	(b) Capt. D. HOGG
Bombing Officer	(a) Lt. F. J. BUTCHER
	(b) Lt. W. B. C. BRANDER (died as result of accident sustained on duty)
	(c) Lt. C. HAUGHTON
Assistant Adjutant	(a) Lt. J. JOHNSTON
	(b) Lt. E. H. THOMAS
	(c) Lt. T. W. SANDERSON
Assistant Quartermaster	(a) Lt. E. H. THOMAS
	(b) Lt. F. C. HUFTON
H.Q. Platoon and Signals Officer	(a) Lt. J. C. SIMPSON
	(b) Lt. O. CARRUTHERS
	(c) Lt. F. C. NOTMAN
Transport Officer	Lt. C. E. TURNER
Gas Officer	(a) Lt. W. H. ROBERTSON, M.C.
	(b) Lt. E. R. KILLICK
Liaison Officer . .	Lt. W. V. PACKE, D.S.O.
Cadet Training Officer	(a) Capt. E. S. ARMSTRONG
	(b) Lt. F. N. HILLIER, M.C.
Ammunition Officer	(a) Capt. D. HOGG
	(b) Lt. W. A. JOHNSTON, M.C.
Security Officer	Lt. R. C. WILLIAMS, M.M.
Bandmaster . . .	Lt. S. J. G. CRAKER
Assistant Signals Officer	Lt. H. POCOCK
Assistant Intelligence Officer	Lt. F. WHITAKER
Assistant Transport Officer	2/Lt. H. GALLOWAY
Sports and Social Officer	(a) 2/Lt. W. R. C. HAMLIN
	(b) Lt. R. S. SHILLINGFORD

A COMPANY

Company Commander .	(a) Major S. BAYLISS SMITH
	(b) Major C. MENPES, M.C.
Second-in-Command	(a) Capt. E. S. ARMSTRONG
	(b) Capt. F. C. DRISKELL

Platoon Commanders	Lt. R. N. ALLEN
	Lt. H. A. HYDE
	Lt. H. SPURDENS
	Lt. A. G. GOODALL
	Lt. R. J. SUTTON
	Lt. R. I. THOMAS
	Lt. W. A. JAMES
	2/Lt. W. R. C. HAMLIN

B COMPANY

Company Commander .	(a) Major A. E. HANSEN, M.C.
	(b) Major E. C. PUPLETT
Second-in-Command	Capt. J. MERRILL
Platoon Commanders	Lt. S. H. C. ROSE
	Lt. F. A. TOTTEM
	Lt. D. J. CARRIE
	Lt. D. HOGG
	Lt. A. G. HANCOCK
	Lt. H. J. STARR

C COMPANY

Company Commander .	Major W. L. HARRILD
Second-in-Command	(a) Capt. R. C. HAWKINS, D.S.O.
	(b) Capt. G. M. BOYD
Platoon Commanders	Lt. C. W. WILLISON
	Lt. J. N. M. CAMPBELL
	Lt. E. A. FILBY
	Lt. E. W. LEWIS
	Lt. T. K. COLLETT
	Lt. C. A. MONKS

D COMPANY

Company Commander	Major G. A. POCOCK, M.C.
Second-in-Command	Capt. W. LEFEAUX
Platoon Commanders	Lt. A. H. WATERS
	Lt. C. M. MONKS
	Lt. C. BARNARD
	Lt. R. B. ROGERS
	Lt. F. H. PERRY

M.G. COMPANY

Company Commander .	(a) Major H. D. REYNOLDS, M.C.
	(b) Major F. W. CASWELL
Second-in-Command	(a) Capt. F. W. CASWELL
	(b) Capt. R. B. DEWSBURY
	(c) Capt. S. D. CLARKE
Platoon Commanders	Lt. F. L. HARRIS
	Lt. W. A. JOHNSTON, M.C.
	Lt. A. S. PULLEY, M.C.
	Lt. H. CHANDLER
	Lt. E. J. AMOS
	Lt. F. G. DOWNING

MOBILE COLUMN

Company Commander .	(a) Capt. T. K. COLLETT
	(b) Capt. S. BAYLISS SMITH

Second-in-Command	Capt. P. S. AYERS, M.C.
Platoon Commanders	Lt. A. S. CLARK
	Lt. E. H. C. LINDLEY
	Lt. S. W. SCARLETT
	Lt. J. N. CAIR
	Lt. L. A. PETTITT

E COMPANY

Company Commander .	(a) Lt. J. JOHNSTON
	(b) Capt. E. S. ARMSTRONG
	(c) Lt. S. F. BAGSHAW
Chief Instructor	Lt. E. D. WALPOLE

ELECTRICITY UNIT

Company Commander	Capt. W. G. TREND
Platoon Commanders	Lt. E. R. SCOTT
	Lt. W. S. COLLINS

TANKS UNIT

Lt. A. SATERFORD
2/Lt. F. C. FEATHERSTONE

The following held office before H.G. Commissions were granted :—

Commanding Officer	F. W. L. HULK
Adjutant . .	G. R. JEFFS, M.S.M.
Engineering Officer	P. W. CRAKER, O.B.E.
Quartermaster	(a) Hon. R. G. WHITELEY, O.B.E.
	(b) H. WHITTAKER
Gas Officer	G. W. HIMUS

A COMPANY

Company Commander	(a) C. H. ROLLSTON	
	(b) H. A. TOSLAND	
Platoon Commanders	A. W. MILLER	E. J. SQUIB
	D. MACKAY	R. W. WEEKES

B COMPANY

Company Commander	(a) J. C. LEWIS, O.B.E.
	(b) E. V. FAIRNEY
Platoon Commander	A. T. COX

C COMPANY

Second-in-Command	(a) F. C. HUFTON
	(b) D. K. RYAN
Platoon Commanders	F. J. STANGER
	T. W. BRIGGS

D COMPANY

Second-in-Command	S. W. JOHNSON
Platoon Commander	V. HEAL, M.C.